RATE-OF-RETURN ANALYTICS

ISBN-13: 978-1530465613
ISBN-10: 1530465613

Dedicated to future generations in hopes that this book might be a useful reference.

TABLE OF CONTENTS

The Return: Overview and Examples

Internal Rate of Return (IRR) in Prior Period Cost

INTRODUCTION

A better understanding of rates of return and pricing may help savers, investors and businesses better manage their finances and avoid losses. Policymakers seeking to boost economic performance may also benefit from analytical tools to prevent policy actions from leading to financial crises and worsening poverty and inequality.

Drawing from five centuries of thought, this book explores a framework for rates of return analysis in hopes of finding solutions to economic and financial dilemmas. When asset price growth outpaces the growth in rates of return on cost (RRC) of financial entities, unsustainable bubble-crash cycles, losses and economic dislocation may result. From a policymaking standpoint, debt-based growth policies are often proposed to stimulate economic activity and boost gains in asset markets. However, when growth in rates of return lag the growth in asset prices, the consequences for indebted businesses and individuals caught up in the boom can be disastrous: Business and bank failures and personal financial hardship for individuals including unemployment, losses on home values and retirement assets. Moreover, wealth inequality may persist when the price growth of assets systematically exceeds the growth in rates of return.

Beyond its application to asset pricing, the concept of rates of return on cost (RRC) may apply to individuals as well. Sources of poverty through declining purchasing power may be traced to a *returns-to-consumer price gap* when consumer prices rise faster than the *rate of return on the cost of living* (RRCOL). Individuals in the pursuit of higher incomes can also avoid potential financial strains by comparing those incomes to associated costs of living.

Summary of Book Structure. The book is divided into three parts which include the Appendices.

Part I develops a framework for a better understanding of rates of return, with definitions and a review of the subject from historical literature spanning five centuries. Beginning with the section on income real estate, a *returns-to-valuation* theory begins to emerge, and in Part II, the analysis is applied to equities.

1

Part II identifies and constructs a measure of rate of return called *rate of return on cost* (RRC), then computes the RRC for publicly-traded non-financial firms in five sectors worldwide with total market capitalization of an estimated U.S. $700 billion as of 2015. In a *returns-to-valuation analysis*, the firms' RRCs are then compared to the growth in their equity prices to detect asset mispricing, either in the form of overvaluation or undervaluation, originating from a theorized *returns-to-valuation gap*.

A rate of return variant for individuals termed *rate of return on cost of living* (RRCOL) is also considered. The concept of a *returns-to-consumer price gap* is introduced in which consumer prices rise faster than the *rate of return on the cost of living* (RRCOL). Such an analytical approach may be applied as a poverty-fighting tool. Part II tentatively concludes with a more general theory of *returns-to-pricing* that suggests that rates of returns of financial entities should roughly align with pricing –in both asset and goods markets.

The appendices also provide extensive supporting information and supplementary historical analyses. The closing summary on future directions includes suggestions for improved analytical approaches for economic management in the 21st century and a guide for reconfiguring GDP to construct a rate of return measure.

Qualifications and Shortcomings. The writing of this book presented a serious challenge as it straddles a number of disciplines including economics, finance and accounting over an extensive historical timeframe during which in many cases the use of language shifted. Some of the elements presented in this book's framework may not exist elsewhere. Therefore, there may be some new and unconventional approaches adopted.

Unraveling the historical literature was at times a difficult task: It is not uncommon to encounter varying definitions for the same or similar terms, varying terms for similar or identical concepts, as well as possible errors, oversights and ambiguities of the authors.

Therefore, the book could be viewed as a draft work-in-progress that further study and collaborative work can improve upon. It is hoped that even if typos, errors, omissions, misinterpretations, or oversimplifications exist, that the essentials still remain. The reader is encouraged to consult other resources and scholars on individual topics to supplement an understanding of the material presented here.

References are from a wide variety of sources, both academic and practitioner-oriented. It is recognized that using non-academic sources may appear to reduce the quality of the research, but this approach is considered preferable so as to identify variations in viewpoints, even subtle ones.

Citation from a particular work of an author does not imply a validation of, or agreement with, much or any of the author's other writings and theories. It is recognized that some citations may be used while entirely disregarding parts of the arguments or passages from which they were taken; even if so, the original meaning of the cited passage is intended to be preserved as best as possible. Concisely summarizing of the vast body of research spanning five centuries is probably an impossible task but it is hoped that enough information has been retained that can improve upon the understanding of rates of return.

Technical parts familiar to readers can be skipped over. For the author, the book also constitutes a collection of various notes and reflections. It is recognized that there may be some occasional digressions due to this author's interest in a particular topic; even if the relevance to *rates of return* may not be entirely obvious, there may be important linkages that could be explored in further research. Conventions adopted in the book are summarized in an Addendum before the References.

There are some modifications from previous books (Kennedy 2014, 2015). For example, the *net cash flow* (NCF) measure (also called *equity income*) from the previous books is now updated to include the modification for *acquisitions* as suggested in Kennedy (2014) but not reflected in the data in that book; accordingly, NCF is now referred to as *net net cash flow* (NNCF). Commentary in the appendices of Kennedy 2015 also has been updated, so that the concept of *return on investment* refers to *rates of return on cost*. The term *economic entity* was previously used without substantial explanation; here, economic entities are defined more precisely as financial entities whose overall activities (revenues, costs and financing aspects) are *voluntary*.

3

PART I

RATES OF RETURN: A FRAMEWORK

The table below shows a general framework for understanding rates of return to be followed throughout the book.

TABLE: RATES OF RETURN FRAMEWORK

CATEGORY	SUB-CATEGORY	Synchronicity: Return, Cost	Rate of Return Examples
1. FINANCIAL ENTITIES			
A	Organization	Synchronous	RRC
B	Individual	Synchronous	RRC (cost of living)
2. ASSETS OF FINANCIAL ENTITY (generating income/savings for financial entities)			
A	Fixed Assets/Assets	FC, Prior Period	IRR, fin. ratios
B	Financial Entity-Org.	FC, Synchronous	IRR, RRC, cap rates
3. ASSETS TO OWNER/INVESTOR(S) AS CAPITAL OF FINANCIAL ENTITY (Income-generating)			
A	Equity	FC, Prior Period	IRR, ROI, fin. ratios, cap rates
B	Debt	FC, Prior Period	IRR, ROI, fin. ratios, cap rates
4. ASSETS: Non-income generating; reliance on future purchasing power			
A	Category #3A #3B	FC, Prior Period	IRR, ROI
B	Other-Various	FC, Prior Period	IRR, ROI

Clarifications.

The "rates of return framework" table above, abbreviated as the "framework table," presents a variety of possible applications of rates of return. The abbreviations in the table are: **FC**: Future Costs (forward-looking decisions); Fin. Ratios is *financial ratios* and in particular *profitability ratios*; "cap rates" is *capitalization rates*; **IRR** is the *internal rate of return* and requires a "purchase price" or *initial cost/outlay*; **ROI** is the *return on investment*; **RRC** is the *rate of return on cost* (return and cost synchronous, rate of return is independent of a decision on an asset purchase); RRC (cost of living) refers to the "personal" *rate of return on the cost of living* (RRCOL) for individuals. **Businesses in Self-Employment**. The businesses of self-employed individuals are viewed as best categorized in #2B because the business is a form of *asset* owned by the individual Any income derived from the self-employment business (wages, distributions/owner draws) provide the individual with an income to be counted as income for an *individual* "financial entity" (#1B). **Real Estate.** Income real estate (whether residential or commercial real estate owned for purposes of income generation) is in Category #2B since income real estate is generally an asset of another financial entity (whether an organization such as a real estate holding company or an individual investor). While an owner-occupied home would be considered an extension of an individual's financial activity (Category #1B), *residential* real estate owned wholly or in part for income-generating purposes has the quality of a financial entity owned by the individual and separate from the individual's own personal finances.

In addition to the above examples of rates of return, *financing cost* (aka *cost of capital*, and more specifically known as the *weighted average cost of capital* or WACC) as a rate of return measure for financial entities-organization may also be added. The financing cost/cost of capital is more appropriately the rate of return to investors in this financial entity's capital, and which is fundamentally distinct from the rate of return *of the financial entity itself*, although it may represent a "hurdle" rate of return for the firm. It should also be emphasized that the *financing cost* is derived by a process of *estimation* and relies on variables including policy interest rates (e.g. the *riskfree* rate) that may introduce distortions to be detailed below, and which may be quite unrelated to firm-specific rates of return.

Comparison with Financial Statements. It might be helpful to map the above framework to financial statements (*balance sheet, income statement and cash flow statement*) in the financial accounting context for a financial entity. For **Category #1** both an income statement and a balance sheet are needed in order to construct a cash flow statement from which rate of return data can be obtained (RRC). **Categories #2, #3 and #4** all correspond to balance sheet items, with #2 on the asset side (left), and #3 and #4 the capital side (right) of the balance sheet—the capital of the financial entity is an *asset* for investors and accounted for separately, see ROI below; **Category #3 or #4** assets are divided according to whether the asset generates current income for investors/owners. **Sub-category #2A**, "fixed assets" are typically are listed as PP&E or similar titling on a balance sheet. As for **Category #2B**, ownership of a financial entity such as a business may be accounted for differently depending on whether a controlling interest is involved or not, but remains an asset of the financial entity. Financial ratios are rates of return that require data from both the income statement and the balance sheet. The ROI does not necessarily require data from a financial statement since the data can be derived from the individual assets owned by the investors. **Category #4** also includes other assets that are unrelated to the capital of a financial entity such as commodities or collectibles, and financial statements as for financial entities are not applicable.

Overview of Framework

The rates of return under study here, unless otherwise stated, may be referred to as *financial r*ates of return.

Categories and Subcategories

As shown in the framework table, the basic framework is divided into **Financial Entities** (Category #1: #1A and #1B) and **Assets** (Categories #2*, #3, #4). Note that financial entities become **assets** in Category #2B). The **sub-categories** as shown in the framework table are below. For financial entities, these are organizations and individuals.

Category #1: Financial Entities

The question arises as to *who* or *what* is generating the rates of return under study. The term "financial entity" is used here to describe human activity that produces, owns or controls some form of income, net of costs. Two types of financial entity are:

1. Organizations (#1A)
2. Individuals (#1B)

Category #1A. Examples of organizational financial entities are businesses/firms, income real estate, organizations such as NPOs, NGOs, churches, governments, and even self-employed individuals as owner/operators of their own business. The term "financial entity" as used here is not synonymous with *financial*

7

institution such as a bank, although banks and other financial institutions can be considered financial entities. An owner of assets such as real estate (whether an individual or a real estate holding company), or other companies can be a financial entity in the sense of controlling income-producing assets.

The term "financial entity" when not qualified most often will refer to organizations as businesses (including income real estate, or self-employment as a business); note that non-profit organizations are examples of organizations that may not use the term "net profit" in their accounting, but that generate a measure of surplus *(fund surplus)* and can even generate sufficient cash flow [*net cash flow* (NCF)] to service debt, for example.

A financial entity is not expected to categorically produce a *positive* net income (net cash flow NCF) at all times, even if this is the intent of the owners or members of the organization. Financial entities have a source of income which is called "revenues" (or sometimes "gross receipts") and the costs related to those revenues are deducted to arrive at a "net benefit." An important distinction which is not always made clear is the difference between *revenues* and *sources of financing* (such as equity or debt financing). Both revenues and financing sources are cash "flowing" into the company and may be easily confused; revenues typically are the result of sales to customers for goods or services, while financing sources are provided by investors who often expect some kind of return on their money, or if a non-profit, contributors/donors who are supporting the organization in some way. In the case of government entities, bonds (debt) are a common source of financing, but equity is usually supplied to the entity through taxation, although tax funds do not currently give taxpayers "ownership rights" to the entity. A third source of financing, provided by central banks, is base (or high-powered) money which involves essentially money creation.

Financial independence. A complication in defining "financial entity" is that some financial entities are in some way highly *dependent* on another entity, or form a part of another financial entity; the lack of independence may render analysis of the dependent entity meaningless. Therefore, *independence* is critical to analysis is to identify whether a portion of revenues or expenses

8

involves large *related-party transactions/relationships* that represent a lack of independence and control. *Customer concentrations* including reliance on revenue from government contracts also should be examined closely. (Kennedy 2015)

Non-Monetary Aspect. The income does not necessarily need to be measured in currency terms (such as Dollars, Yen, Euros, etc.); for example, an individual Robinson Crusoe on an island can be a financial entity. The "income" generated is what is produced to survive through fishing, hunting, scavenging, etc. (e.g. number of fish caught per day, nuts collected, etc.); any "surplus" left over at the end of the day after consumption is a form of *savings* or *net benefit*. A money-less or barter commune/community is still a financial entity in which the individual members voluntarily produce goods or services in exchange for other goods or services.

Category #1B: Individuals. Individuals are also considered financial entities in the sense that they have a source (or multiple sources) of income and their expenditures are their personal "cost of living." Although the focus here is on businesses/organizations, the concept of rates of return is believed to be applicable to individuals as well. For example, "costs" in a business context can be applied to individuals as the "cost of living." The topic of individual or "personal" *rates of return on cost of living* (RRCOL) will be addressed in the section on possible applications in Part II.

Economic Entity as Extension of Financial Entity. A "financial entity" could be described as an "economic entity" when the condition of *voluntary activity* is added, as noted in Appendix 1.

Assets (Category #2 through #4)

Category #2A. The broadest term for assets of a financial entity is *total assets*, which can be the basis for certain financial ratio measures of returns, such as the ROA (return on assets).

A sub-category of the total assets is *fixed assets*, also referred to by other names including *Plant, Property and Equipment* (PP&E), "capital stock," and sometimes simply as "capital." Note that real estate, if non-income generating where the financial entity occupies its own building(s) and plants the real estate is not considered to be income-generating (although it is possible for some of the space to be leased out to others, and therefore to be separated out as a separate income real estate portion of the asset).

Category #2B. A financial entity itself (organization) can also be an income-generating asset of another financial entity (for example, a company or individual buy a business, or income real estate). The capital of a financial entity (equity and debt) is simultaneously an asset to owners and investors. Equity interests may or may not pay out dividends/distributions. In the event they do, Category #3A applies. Interest-paying debt is Category #3B. As for assets that do not generate (current) income and rely on future purchasing power, see Category #4.

Assets of Individuals (Category #2) Rates of return not only exist for businesses contemplating an investment in an asset, but can apply to individuals as well. When a homeowner is asked to incur a cost (pay an installation fee) in order to receive a future stream of benefits; these benefits include a cost *savings* of the homeowner, and therefore an increased *net benefit*. For example, installation of insulation materials to reduce home heating/cooling bills, or installation of a solar power system to reduce energy costs in the future.

Distinguishing between consumer goods and assets of individuals may need to be evaluated on a case-by-case basis. For example purchase of a car for commuting may be directly related to increasing one's income to commute to a new employer; a house could function partly as an asset if while living in the home a room is rented out.

Assets to Investors as Capital of the Financial Entity –Income-Generating (Category #3). The two primary assets that are capital of the financial entity that can generate income for investors in those assets are:

1. Equities (equity securities)
2. Debt (including bonds, loans, etc.)

For equity securities, *current income* to investors (if paid) is dividends/distributions; for debt securities (e.g. bonds), current income is interest (plus return of principal originally lent).

Clarification: Concept of "Total Return"- Category Split (#3 and #4). When we hear "The return on ABC company's stock last year was 10%," this is usually refers to a measure of rate of return on investment popularly called the *total return*. This *total return* may more formally be called a type of *return on investment* (ROI), as will be detailed elsewhere. The total return consists of both the current income (e.g. dividends) from that stock to investors, as well as any *capital appreciation*; when the security is sold, any profit (difference between buying and selling price) may be referred to as a *capital gain*. Therefore, Category #3 and Category #4 may refer to the *same* security, but one portion of the income is from current income generation (Category #3), and another portion is from future purchasing power (appreciation) (Category #4). For debt securities (e.g. bonds), the total return consists of both the capital appreciation and the interest as the current income. (Peters 2008: 28)

In the context of discounted cash flow analysis (DCF), Irving Fisher (1930) made a distinction between capital gain and present income as well. He states: "It is not uncommon for economic students to make the mistake of including capital gains as income....Capital gains, as already implied, are merely capitalization of future income. They are never present income...." (25)

Other Assets. Reliance on Future Purchasing Power (Category #4). This category refers to assets that rely on future purchasing power. Examples of assets include cash/currencies, collectibles, precious metals, futures and options; also applies to the capital appreciation portion of securities (debt and equity) as noted above. **Consumer Price Deflation**. Increased purchasing power can be achieved by the value of the particular asset increasing relative to prices of consumer goods/services. This includes consumer price deflation – that is if the prices of consumer goods and services declines relative to the price of an asset in this category, the asset has "appreciated" relative to consumer prices. Although this category does not include ongoing future cash inflows, there can be a future cash inflow from the sale of the asset. **Market Assessment**. Since Category #4 assets do not generate current income, it should be recognized that the return to investors in the form of future purchasing power/capital appreciation tends to originate from evaluation of the company's performance and prospects by investors, analysts and the so-called "market", and may not *necessarily* be causally connected to the internal, recurring, equity income generation by the firm—significant divergences are possible, especially in bubble markets. Policy interest rates also may be another predominantly external source impacting upon prices of securities, whether equities or bonds. Capital gains on bonds can also arise from changes in policy interest rates (Kennedy 2015, see "policy interest rates").

As an asset (Category #2) of another financial entity, a business itself (i.e. 100% ownership of the equity of a firm) could be sold for a capital gain (Category #4). However, the source of the gain may not be causally connected to better performance of the firm – simply that the buyer of the business purchases the business at a price higher than the seller/previous owner's purchase price, perhaps because the buyer highly values the prospects of the firm in the future; 2.

For investors and retirees, a final point might be added regarding reliance upon capital gains as a source of income rather than dividends: "...dividends, through both yield and growth, enable investors to meet real-world financial needs directly with their portfolios. Fickle capital gains (green today, red tomorrow, endlessly unpredictable) do not." (Peters: 205)

Other Assets (Category #4). There are innumerable other types of assets that that are not part of the capital of a financial entity that are bought and sold, some as investments, and some as hobbies. These types of assets can include precious metals*, art, antiques and other collectibles including comic books and baseball cards.

It might be pointed out that precious metals are mined and become assets when sold into the market. While the prices of the metals may in some way be related to the intensity of production and the profitability of the mining companies, the metals themselves do not represent the equity or liabilities of the entities mining them.

Exceptional Case: Capital Gains Dominant in Business Model (Category #1 or #4). If a company's primary business model relies largely upon *capital gains on asset sales* for its *recurring* source of revenues (e.g. an investment company which buys and sells assets), then it may be unclear whether the rate of return to be computed should be categorized in **Category #1** (as a separate financial entity) or **Category #4** (an asset relying upon future purchasing power/capital appreciation). The answer may in part depend on the relative size of the assets (to revenues/sales). To cite an extreme example, if a financial entity trades a single massive asset once a year for a capital gain which constitutes 100% of the business revenues, the Category #4 rate of return may appear to make more sense than Category #1. However, since there are likely to be operating costs associated with the business even if a single massive capital gain is their only "product", Category #1 would still be a reasonable categorization in order to capture all of the costs of the business activities. Nevertheless, a thorough analysis of the financial entity would require an analysis of that underlying asset sold.

Concept: Synchronicity of return and cost

Rates of return can be classified by synchronicity of cost relative to the return. There are three types of *return-cost synchronicity*, one synchronous, one asynchronous, and one a mix of both, in that the asynchronicity is "corrected" by discounting.

1. Synchronous (time period of return and cost matched)
2. Prior Period (Sunk) Costs (asynchronous)
3. Future Costs (Forward-Looking) (both)

For the **"synchronous"** category, the time period of the return matches that of the cost. **Example:** For a synchronous (return and cost both in same period) rate of return, the return in that period (say fiscal year 2015) is expected to match the cost for that same period (fiscal year 2015). The *same period costs* of investment such as *capital expenditures* are made within the same time period as the return (such as fiscal year 2015)—these capital expenditures are *additions* to *prior period investment costs*.

The rate of return associated with synchronous return and costs is the *rate of return on cost* (RRC) for organizations, and for individuals, a rate of return on *cost of living*, to be detailed elsewhere in the book.

For the **Prior Period Costs** category, the costs were incurred in a prior period, that is, a period before the return was generated; there is a time "mismatch" or time lag between the cost and the return.

Prior period costs also can be referred to as "sunk" as they cannot be recovered. For example, the return (say, net cash flow or profit) of an entity is generated in fiscal year 2015; prior period costs would be those costs that were incurred prior to fiscal year 2015. Capital investments recorded on the balance sheet of a firm are typically called "Plant, Property & Equipment", "fixed capital" "fixed assets" or a similar titling.

This fixed capital can be a mix of both *same period* and *prior period* costs. For example, the profit for fiscal year 2015 is compared to the balance sheet item such as "PP&E" as measured on December 31, 2015. For a company in business for more than a few years, much of the cost on the balance sheet may have been incurred prior to fiscal year 2015, and some portion during fiscal year 2015. In contrast, for a start-up business with a history of a year or less, its assets and fixed capital would involve synchronous costs and returns (same time period).

In a macroeconomic sense, prior period costs of investment (or a mix of same period and prior period) also can be accounted for as what is called "fixed capital formation" or "capital stock" of a nation, for example.

The applicable rate of return for Prior Period Costs depends on the objective: For decision-making purposes, the *internal rate of return* (IRR) to be discussed below in "Future Costs" is appropriate. For Category #2A, *profitability ratios* are often employed as a measure of returns. For Category #3 and #4, the *return on investment* (ROI) is also a simple and popular tool for evaluating historical returns. All of these types of rate of return will be discussed further elsewhere.

Future costs typically involve *decision-making* and the rate of return is not known until the (future) cost/investment is made (represented by a purchase/selling price). The applicable rate of return for an asset purchase is generally the internal rate of return (IRR) or variation. See DCF analysis elsewhere for more detail. The steps can be summarized simply as follows:

Purchase Price (Cost) Known →IRR

Future costs are a mix of asynchronous and synchronous return to costs: Asynchronous in that an initial outlay (the cost or amount

14

of the investment) is followed by a (forecasted) stream of future net cash flows; synchronous in the sense that through the process of *discounting* using a *discount rate* (which is a rate of return), the stream of future cash flows can be brought to the present (i.e. present value or PV), and therefore "synchronized" with the initial cost outlay, to determine whether the investment is worthwhile.

The term "future costs" is used to indicate two types of cost: First, the decision is about the initial cost to be made in the future, and second, the future forecasted cash flows are "net" of the *future costs* associated with them, that is, *net cash flows*.

Since the future involves an element of uncertainty, the term "expected" (as in *expected return*) is often used when referring to future costs in conjunction with uncertainty; the computation is made with a *discount rate* – to be explained further in the topics of *discounted cash flow* (DCF) analysis, uncertainty and risk.

Rates of Return for Financial Entities
For financial entities, there are two types of rate of return, one is organizational, and the other is for individuals:
1. Rate of Return on Cost (organizational)
2. Rate of Return on Cost of Living (individuals)

In both cases, the cost and return are synchronous (same time period).

The focus of this book is on the rates of return generated by the *financial entity* (#1A) as an organization.

The RRC, or rate of return on cost, is a rate of return of financial entities that exists *independently* of a decision being made as to the purchase (selling) price of the asset or the required rate of return by an investor. The rate of return on cost is the focus of Part II of the book. Analysis of the financial entity and its *equity income* can provide important insights as to:

1. The firm's capacity to generate income for equity holders, either *potential* equity income for investors if dividends/distributions are not paid, or *realized* if there are such payments (Kennedy 2014).
2. The firm's capacity to service its obligations to lenders/debt holders ("debt service capacity"). (Kennedy 2015).

Rates of Return as Measure of Historical Performance

This section attempts to clarify the concept of *rates of return* for financial entities in the context of analyzing the past performance of a business or equity investment. The key distinction between rates of return for financial entities and rates of return on assets is explained.

Business owners, including self-employed individuals, as well as investors considering buying/selling an existing business (including income real estate) or an equity investment may wish to have an idea of how the entity has performed historically. However, when thinking about past "performance," it may not be entirely clear what *rate of return measure* would be applicable.

Comparison of Financial Entity Performance (Category #1A). How has the existing business performed over the years relative to other businesses? Financial analysis is used to produce all sorts of measures of performance*, and these should not be ignored. However, for *rates of return* that apply to performance of a business, **Category #1A**, Financial Entity-Organization in the framework table above would apply. However, in the section below, it is possible to treat the *internal rate of return* (IRR) in a historical context, with limitations as will be noted. An IRR case study with historical data is also attempted.

The *rate of return on cost* (RRC) is a measure of performance of financial entities that is the focus of Part II of this book, and for which the groundwork was presented in Kennedy 2014 and 2015.

*For example, it is common to compute profitability as a measure of performance, but as is noted elsewhere that profitability (defined as net profit/revenue %) is not a rate of return measure.

Distinction: Financial Entity vs. Asset Rates of Return. At this juncture, it is important to clarify that rates of return of financial entities are distinct from the rate of returns on *assets* (Categories #2,#3,#4) which include assets of a financial entity (#2A,B), whether income-producing or not (#3,#4). Recall that category #3 is *capital* of the entity as well as being an asset to investors by the financial accounting identity A=L+E.

To illustrate the distinction, let's consider the case of a financial entity sale. Owners of a financial entity (organization) may end up selling 100% of the entity *itself* as an asset. Which rate of return applies? Is it the rate of return of the firm *itself* or the rate of return on the firm as an *asset* to the investor/buyer (i.e. its equity capital, 100% ownership)? Since the buying-selling of a business depends upon a *decision* about an initial cost outlay, the rate of return is not known until the actual purchase takes place. Once that purchase price is known, (i.e. the cost to the investor/purchaser), then the rate of return can be calculated using the IRR as stated above. Once the transaction takes place firm becomes an asset of another financial entity (such as a wholly-owned subsidiary), either another organization or an individual who buys the business (Category #2).

It is acknowledged that if an investor/buyer has a decided upon a *required rate of return*, it could be argued that the rate of return *is* in fact known ahead of time; however in practice it is likely that the actual rate of return would still be subject to any final negotiations. For example, an investor's required rate of return might be 10% but when the transaction is completed, the rate of return as calculated by the IRR might end up varying somewhat from 10%, lower or higher.

Rate of Return on Cost of Living (individuals). In addition to a rate of return on cost for organizations, individuals are also presumed to have a "personal" rate of return on their cost of living. Essentially this means any amounts saved from their gross income divided by total living costs. This is not the same as a cost of living index; the cost of living should reflect actual expenditures of individuals and households. The Rate of Return on Cost of Living (RRCOL) is detailed in Part II.

Applicability of Other Rate of Return Measures to Financial Entities

A question might arise why the rate of return for financial entities shouldn't be (a) the *internal rate of return* (IRR); (b) the *financing costs* used as *the discount rate* in DCF analysis such as the *weighted average cost of capital* (WACC; or (c) capitalization rates as used in valuation of various assets including equities and real estate. These measures of rates of return are briefly overviewed here are detailed further in the section on Future Costs.

Measure #1: Internal Rate of Return (IRR)

Financial Entity: Established Going Concern. IRR is typically applied when an initial cost outlay is followed by a future stream of income (net cash flows), such as for a project, investment in equipment, and asset purchases such as in bond pricing.

There is some question as to the applicability of the IRR approach with established *going concern* entities* since the initial cost "starting point" may be difficult to determine. An exercise computing the historical IRR of an actual financial entity (consumer goods firm) is attempted in the section on Future Costs and IRR.

Business Start-Up/Venture. When the financial entity is a *business start-up* being considered, future cost decision-making is involved in evaluating the rate of return. The asset is the equity investment (*initial capital contribution*) in the start-up, which is the *initial cost outlay* in computing the IRR. The future stream of net cash flows would need to be forecast by the analyst. Recall that the resulting IRR is based on the equity investment as an *asset*, and would not produce a rate of return *for the entity itself.*

Historical Performance. For evaluation of past performance of such an equity investment (i.e. asset) in a start-up after the fact (ex post), the rate of return that applies is the IRR for an asset; see the previous commentary on Comparison of Asset Performance. For evaluation of performance of a start-up many years after the founding of the company, and assuming there is sufficient historical data, see the previous commentary on IRR as applied to a *going concern* financial entity. A case study involving IRR is also presented later. Note however the limitations; a number of years of historical data is necessary and evaluating a start-up rate of return using IRR after only a few years may not yield meaningful results.

Measure #2: Financing Costs Applied to Valuation Analysis. The financing costs (also called the "cost of capital") are employed as a tool in valuation analysis: The *discount rate* such as the *weighted average cost of capital* (WACC) is estimated, then the forecasted future net cash flows are discounted by that rate in order to arrive at a measure of present value (PV). The steps in valuation are summarized as follows:

#1 Estimation of discount rate (e.g. WACC)

#2 Computation of Present Value (PV)

Once the purchase price (cost or initial outlay) is known, then the Net Present Value* (NPV) can be computed as follows:

$$NPV = PV - Cost$$

Note that the NPV represents the *return* on the particular investment and is *not* the rate of return. The estimated *discount rate* as noted in Step #1 is a *rate of return* to the investors providing the financing, also referred to as the *cost of capital*.

It is important to emphasize that this *estimated* rate of return is a cost of financing which is distinct from the rate of return *of the financial entity itself*:

The financing costs are derived from the cost of the equity and debt that are used in the financing of the entity. Moreover, financing costs tend to be linked to *policy interest rates*, raising concerns as to correct valuations (such as overvaluations when interest rates are lowered) as detailed elsewhere.

Measure #3: Capitalization Rates. Capitalization rates are another measure of rate of return explored in the section on Future Costs but do not represent rates of return for financial entities. They too are based on estimates as will be shown later.

Rates of Return: Basic Definitions

Rates of return that are the primary emphasis of this book are those calculated for a financial entity as an organization (Category #1A-businesses and organizations including businesses in self-employment and income real estate). Definition of the rate of return for individuals (rate of return on cost of living or RRCOL) will be detailed in Part II.

Rates of return define a relationship between two variables and can be expressed as a ratio and a percentage. In essence, there are two basic and interrelated component variables to this relationship: net benefit and cost, as follows:

$$r = Net\ benefit\ /\ Cost$$

…where r is the rate of return for a single, independent financial entity.

In a simple example, if in 2016 gross sales are 110 and costs are 100, the *net benefit* is 110-100=10. The *rate of return* (over that time period) would be 10/100 or 10% in 2016.

Note: The *net benefit* (numerator) and *cost* (denominator) can be thought of as directionally *opposite* flows in a *capital budgeting* sense: For instance, in the internal rate of return (IRR) computation, an initial cost outlay (*negative*) is followed by a (*positive*) future stream of net cash (in) flows.

Ownership of the Return

Although seemingly obvious but easily overlooked, the *return* (i.e. net benefit) is assumed to be causally linked to, and benefiting the entity or individual that *incurs the cost*. Legal ownership is also assumed, unless contractual arrangements would specify otherwise.

Use of Language

The rate of return relationship also can be verbalized in popular language as "what do I *get* for what I *give up?*"

Rates of return can be abbreviated as "returns" in the framework of this book. The language surrounding rates of return can be confusing: In the literature the usage is mixed: The "returns" in the *plural* form may sometimes refer to the *return* itself (i.e. the numerator in the rate of return relationship) but not as the *ratio* (*rate* of return). Other references to "returns" may mean "rates of return." The term "rates" of return (plural) is preferred over the singular "rate" of return to emphasize that there are *numerous* rates of return in an economy, corresponding to the numerous financial entities that generate rates of return according to market conditions and the capabilities of management.

A rate of return can be positive, zero or negative. For entities that have consistently *negative* rates of return some form of outside financing (debt, equity) is expected to keep them operating, since they are incapable of supporting themselves from the revenues they generate less their costs.

Variables

The variables within the rate of return relationship are: Net benefit, cost, and gross revenues. To recap, *net benefit is the return* and is the numerator; cost is in the denominator, and gross revenues less the cost is equal to the return (net benefit). The term "net benefit" is used because it clarifies that there the return is a "net" figure (net of costs).

Numerator: Return (Net Benefit). The net benefit in the numerator is the *return* (in the singular form) itself (not the *rate* of return), and is normally *net* of costs incurred to obtain that benefit. The *net benefit* (return) can be broken down as follows:

Return = Gross Revenues* – Cost

"Net" Concept. The return should be expressed as *net* or *net of costs*, such as "*net* profit" or "*net* cash flow." For financial entities, "net" means that costs are deducted from *gross revenues/sales** (aka "gross receipts") to arrive at the net figure. It should be emphasized that this net benefit is derived *from gross revenues** of the firm (sales to customers/clients) and *not from financing sources* such as equity issuance or debt.

*Note: Gross revenues (gross sales or gross income) are generated from sales to customers in a financial sense (accrual or cash basis). The costs deducted from these gross revenues to calculate the net benefit are from the *same period* as the net benefit (therefore net benefit for fiscal year 2015 should be net of the costs for 2015). The accounting entries for revenues can be divided into *cash sales* and *sales on credit*, shown below respectively:

Cash Sales
Cash................................x

        Revenues..........................x
Sales on Credit
Accounts Receivable...............x

        Revenues.........x

The Return (as Numerator): Sub-Classifications

Before looking at rates of return, this section reviews the return only (i.e. the "net benefit" or numerator of the rate of return relationship shown above). There are three major classifications of *the return*:

"Net Benefit" Measure (Revenues minus Cost): Net profit (net income), net cash flow (NCF), net surplus, or residual income.*

Output or yield (typically towards a profit maximizing point)

Net Present Value (NPV) in Discounted Cash Flow Analysis.
NPV is the *return* of a future stream of net cash flows (net of costs) discounted to the present by a *discount rate*; the element of uncertainty may be added into the computation; also see *discount rate* in the discussion of rates of return.

Special Note: Output as Return. In economics, output can be considered as a form of return. However, the *output* could refer to the amount(s) produced (yield), *gross* or *net* of costs. Depending upon the reference, it is not always clear whether the entity (or individual farmer, for example) produces the output with any net surplus left over (e.g. net benefit or net profit) *after* costs of production. Part of microeconomic analysis (producer microeconomics) introduces profit *maximization* at various levels of output and costs. On a macro-economic level, for measures of national output (such as GDP), national income accounting suggests that the return (net benefit) is a form of *gross profit*; see Appendix 7 for details.

Financing Activity Separate from Return: Financing Inflows.
It should be emphasized that the *return* does not include inflows from *financing* such as borrowings or equity issuance/capital contributions. Cash *inflows* from loans, equity issuance, and capital contributions are considered separately from the rate of returns relationship because they relate to assets that are the capital of the financial entity (Category #3 from the framework). These *financing* items that are the amounts contributed by investors (e.g. bonds, capital contributions, equity issuance) intended *to generate a return for those who contribute the capital* (the equity or debt holders) --whether from dividends/distributions (equity) or from interest (debt), and not to the business itself.

Denominator: Cost

The denominator is a measure of cost. Historically, costs refer to the *costs of production* for an entity over a defined time period, such as a year or fiscal year. These costs are ultimately physically represented by *cash outflows* from the entity, since ultimately the return (to equity holders or lenders) is to be paid in a physical form such as cash. Using terminology from financial accounting, costs

22

as outflows include: Cost of Goods Sold (COGS) or Cost of Sales (COS), wages/employee compensation, selling, general and administrative expenses (S, G&A), taxes, capital expenditures and acquisitions.

These cost outflows do not include outflows for *financing* purposes such as debt service or dividends/ distributions, or stock buybacks.

Financing Activity Separate from Cost: Financing Outflows. The outflows due to payments of *principal* and *interest* (P+i), *dividends/distributions* are also considered separately from cost as these payment outflows represent a return for those who contribute their capital (the equity or debt holders) --whether in the form of dividends/distributions (equity) or from interest (debt). Recall that this relates to the return in Category #3 from the framework above. Although interest is an expense of the business, it remains a component of the *return* to debtholders, not to the business.

Note that in the finance literature these payment outflows are typically counted as returns to others (for example, *dividends* to equity holders/owners, and *interest* to lenders); the finance literature often focuses on these types of returns to (equity, debt) investments.

Profitability Pitfall: Key Distinction from Rate of Return. The term "profitability" defined as *net income / revenues*, is not a rate of return measure because the denominator of the relationship is *revenues* and not cost. The net profit ratio is expressed as follows:

Net Profit % = Net Profit/Revenues

This measure is not a rate of return measure there the productive activities of the firm/organization are not clearly identified.

There are other definitions using "profits" in the context of "rates of profit" that would be considered rates of return; these are classified and detailed elsewhere.

RATES OF RETURN IN HISTORICAL PERSPECTIVE (16th Century-Present)

This section surveys economic and financial commentary relating to the topic of rates of return. The resources date from approximately 1544 to the present. Adam Smith's 1776 magnum opus, *An Inquiry into the Nature and Causes of the Wealth of Nations* remains a central reference, not only for the information contained therein, but for subsequent debates and discussions his writings stimulated, notably from David Ricardo and John Stuart Mill. Note that citing a particular author is not intended to be a validation of, or an indication of agreement with, the entire body of thought of that particular author. Passages were in some instances taken from expositions unrelated to rates of return, and therefore could be considered as having been taken out of context. This was unavoidable since it was difficult to locate substantial commentary specifically on the subject of rates of return. It is acknowledged that due to changes in language over time as well as where translations were involved, there may be some lack of clarity in certain passages cited; the best interpretation possible is made.

This section begins with historical references to the "return," that is the numerator or "net benefit" of the rate of return relationship.

Following this, the section is organized by synchronicity. Recall the classification of rates of return by the synchronicity of return and cost as follows:
1. Synchronous (time period of return and cost matched)
2. Prior Period (Sunk) Costs (asynchronous)
3. Future Costs (Forward-Looking Decisions) (both)

The Return: Overview and Examples

As stated above in the section on variables, the *return* (not the rate of return) is the numerator of the rate of return relationship and can be divided into three basic types: 1. Net benefit (various) 2. Output/yield 3. Net present value (NPV).

Profit. The term profit is the abbreviation for "net profit" since profit is net of costs. Profit can be *accrual basis* as *cash basis* in an accounting sense. Profit/net profit can be used interchangeably with "net earnings," or "earnings." There are numerous variations of profit; a common variation of the computation of profit in financial analysis is *earnings before interest and taxes*

(EBIT). Other terms for profit include *residual income*, with the entrepreneur/owner of a business that receives the income a residual income *recipient*. In the *residual-dividend model*, the *residual earnings* are the earnings that are not needed for reinvestment in order to maintain the company's target capital structure.

Return in Productive Activity. In the early 20th century, Ludwig von Mises, in describing the process of valuation and system of computation by value in an economic system of private ownership of the means of production, refers to the return in the context of producers: "As a producer he puts goods of a higher order into such use as produces the greatest return." (1920:20)

Profit and Incentives. In one of the earlier references to profit in the context of policy, Sir Thomas Smith in 1549 (later likely published under his son's name, W.S. or William Smith in 1581), uses the term "advantage" as in "every man will seek where the most advantage is." (Hutchison: 20) Smith, within an argument for mercantilism, encourages government policy to "guide" rather than suppress the powerful force of the profit motive, since "…that thing which is profitable to each man by himself, so it be not prejudicial to any other, is profitable to the whole Commonweal" (Ibid)

Output and Profit, Net of Cost. Although the term may not have appeared as *return* or *profit*. Petty (1662) in his analyses of taxation identifies a *surplus* that could be described as such (Hutchison citing Hull (1899); Hutchison: 34, 421). Petty identifies the "true rent" of the land for that year as the "remainder" of the corn after all *expenditures* (being "…his seed out of the proceeds of his harvest, and also what himself hath both eaten and given to others in exchange for clothes and other natural necessaries…"). In valuing the equivalence between corn and silver, this *"rent* or *corn surplus"* is defined as what is *saved* "…the money, which another single man can save, within the same time, over and above his expense, if he employed himself wholly to produce and make it." (Hutchison: 34)

In this case, the return could be defined as an *output* or *yield* (in the form of corn), or it could be a *profit* (in the form of the corn, sold at the market value of the corn, net of the expenditures noted).

Rent as a Form of Profit, Net of Cost (Real Estate and Land).
Historically, the term "rent" referred to a net benefit (net of expenses) derived from real estate/land, as well as a payment to a property owner.   Malthus defined rent as "...the return to landowners after other costs of production had been met, which meant that the proximate cause of rent was the excess of food prices over cost of production." (Winch: 69 citing Malthus in *An Inquiry into the Nature and Progress of Rent* 1815)

The contractual complexities in agricultural production arrangements (farmers/sharecroppers/landowners) aside, this earlier definition of *rent* might correspond to a form of profits on real estate (including land), net of all operating expenses, such as *Net Operating Income* or NOI.

For the purposes of this book, the term rent in the classical sense described above can be viewed simply as another form of *profit* or *net cash flow*, in the context of real estate (including land). Moreover, the term can be confusing as *rent* in the modern business sense tends to mean the gross payment that a tenant (or a lessee) makes to a landlord or lessor (owner of property).

Free Cash Flow, net of Cost. A common measure of return is also *free cash flow* (FCF), defined typically as cash flow from operations less capital spending [Dorsey (2004), Moody's (2000), Rosenbaum and Pearl (2013)].

Dorsey's formula for free cash flow is *cash flow from operations* less *capital spending* (90).   Rosenbaum and Pearl is Earnings before interest and after taxes (EBIAT) + Depreciation and Amortization − Capex − increase/ (decrease) in net working capital (2013: 131, 163).

Hitchner (2011) uses the term *net cash flow* or *net free cash flow* (both abbreviated as NCF).   His formula for NCF is: Earnings before interest and taxes − taxes on EBIT at effective tax rate + depreciation − capital expenditures plus/minus changes in working capital. (2001:500). NCF is also adopted in Kennedy (2014) although an alternative source of NCF is obtained from the *Cash Flow Statement* of a company's financial statements: *Net cash from operations* (NCO) less *capital expenditures* (from the Investing section of the cash flow statement).   NCO may also be termed "net cash provided from/used in operations."   In a

26

proposed extension to the analysis, NCF is modified to deduct cash outflows for *business acquisitions* (acquisitions, net of cash) to arrive at a more comprehensive measure for NCF. (Kennedy 2014: 11) This more comprehensive measure of NCF is termed NNCF in this book, to be detailed in Part II of this book.

Although Dorsey does not relate free cash flow to a particular type of investment, he notes a *free cash flow to sales ratio* of more than 5 percent as being a solid indicator of excess cash generation (Dorsey 91). Kennedy (2014) also computes this ratio as the *net cash flow ratio* (NCF ratio) in the analysis of the *equity income generating capacity* of firms. For the 32 non-financial firms examined over the period, averages of the NCF ratio ranged from -0.01% (oil and gas production) to as high as 42% (computer software: programming/internet) (22-85).

Note that in this book, the NCF ratio from Kennedy (2014) is further adjusted for the *cost of acquisitions*, and this adjusted *equity income* figure is labelled the NNCF ratio, to be detailed in Part II.

Net Present Value as a measure of return will be discussed in further detail elsewhere under Future Costs.

Rates of Return: Overview and Examples

This section divides historical examples of rates of return into three parts according to synchronicity of the return and cost as described above: Synchronous (i.e. "same period"), prior period (sunk) costs, and future costs (forward-looking decisions). Each individual example will be prefaced with a summary of the return measure it represents, as well as the cost; "production" as a cost refers to "production cost" or "cost of production."

Synchronous (Same Period) Rates of Return

Synchronous rates of return are presented here beginning with *output* as a form of return, followed by measures of *profit/net cash flow* as another form of return. Special mention is made of the law of accelerating returns, in which output is described by chip speed.

Return: Output; **Cost:** Production

Three examples of return as *output* (or *yield* as in agriculture) are provided:

Serra. One of the earliest references to returns is found in an Italian writer Antonio Serra [*A Brief Treatise on the Causes which can make Gold and Silver Plentiful in Kingdoms where there are No Mines* (1613)], who in supporting mercantilism argues that increasing returns can be attained in industry relative to agriculture. While in agriculture production could be expanded from 100 to only 150 bushels, in industry "it is just the other way, since they may be multiplied not only two-fold but two hundred-fold and with proportionately less expense." (Hutchison 1988: 19)

Turgot. Anne Robert Jacques Turgot (1727-81), in an essay concerning agricultural production [*Observations on a Paper by Saint-Peravy* (1767)], addresses the issue of diminishing marginal returns, relating additional expenditures to returns. Turgot states essentially that beyond a certain point "...all further expenditure would be useless, and that such increases could even become detrimental." He continues, with figures, "...in the case of ordinary good cultivation, the annual advances return 250 for 100, it is more than likely that as the advances are increased gradually past this point up to the point they return nothing, each increase would be less and less productive." (Hutchison 1988: 317)

J.S. Mill. John Stuart Mill (1848: Book IV *Principles of Political Economy*) also details returns in improvements in agricultural production defined as *output* related to the cost of production. Mill compares three plots of land in which the yield would double "...at only double the expense, and therefore without any increase of the cost of production." (1988: 86-87) Later in the same book in his critique of a passage of Adam Smith's Wealth of Nations (1776) Mill relates returns to expenses: "...the expenses of every producer have diminished as much as his returns." (1988: 88)

Measures of (Net) Profit/Cash Flow to Cost. The following examples center on same-period return and cost where the return is measured by either *(net) profit* or *net cash flow* (NCF), and cost is cost of production.

Return: Profit/Loss **Cost:** Production.
Luis Saravia de la Calle (1544) of the School of Salamanca explains how profit is not guaranteed (Hutchison: 15). The hoped-for price may not materialize to compensate for the costs of production and risk: "If we had to consider labour and risk in order to assess the just price, no merchant would ever suffer loss." (Hutchison 15, citing Grice-Hutchinson 1952 81-2) The "just price" could also be viewed as a price determined by market forces: In the same passage (translated), this "just" price "…arises from the abundance or scarcity of goods, merchants, and money,…, and not from costs, labour and risk."(15)

Return: Profits **Cost:** Production (cost of living reference). David Ricardo (1821) also makes reference to the impact of costs of production on profits, specifically the cost of labor (wages): "…for nothing can affect profits but a rise in wages; silks and velvets are not consumed by the labourer, and therefore cannot raise wages." (118) Ricardo links the *cost of living* of workers to their wages, as follows "The necessity which the labourer would be under of paying an increased price for such necessaries, would oblige him to demand more wages; and whatever increases wages, necessarily reduces profits." (118)

Return: Profits **Cost:** Production.
In agriculture, John Stuart Mill uses Smith's own example and the *rate of profit* in the new colonies to explain a relationship between profit and production costs. "When the most fertile and best situated lands have been all occupied, less profit can be made by the cultivators of what is inferior both in soil and situation." (J.S. Mill, quoting Smith 90) Here, the reader is reminded of Malthus' law of diminishing returns (Winch: 69, citing Malthus 1815).
On the topic of "the tendency of profits to a minimum," Mill critiques Smith's "competition between different capitals" (Smith 316) explanation for depressing prices and profits. While both authors would agree that lower prices for producers (assuming expenses are unchanged) would lower their profits, Mill identifies a scenario in which lower producer expenses could coincide with lower prices/revenues that would not necessarily result in a fall in profits: Should *all* commodities simultaneously fall in price

"...the expenses of every producer have diminished as much as his returns." (88) Note that this passage is highlighted as an example the meaning of *returns* which suggests *gross receipts* or *revenues* (price x quantity sold of goods) of the producers. Mill then suggests that one source of production cost – wages of labour—could explain why profits have fallen, rather than the fall of prices. (88)

Mill emphasizes the importance of "improvements in production" relative to other industries, and on the cost of production in various industries. In the textile industry (spun and woven fabrics are noted), improvements in production "...greater than have taken place in the production of the precious metals..." will see their prices fall. "Other things, again, instead of falling, have risen in price, because their cost of production, compared with that of gold and silver*, has increased. Among these are all kinds of food...." (89)

Note that gold and silver were mined and used as money at the time.

Rate of Return on Cost (RRC)
Return: NNCF **Cost:** Production (Cash Flow)

The *rate of return on cost* (RRC) is a measure developed in this book and is the focus of Part II. RRC is defined as *Net Cash Flow net of acquisitions* (or "net net cash flow", NNCF) divided by the same period cost of production (as a cash outflow). The term should not be confused with *rate of return over cost* (Fisher 1930). RRC is synchronous, with the time period being the same fiscal year.

Laws of Returns

Two laws of returns are reviewed briefly here with the general assumption that the return and the related costs are *approximately* synchronous since this assumption may not apply in all cases of these laws.

The Law of Diminishing Returns. Thomas Malthus and Edward West (1815) are famous for the *law of diminishing returns* which had particular relevance in agriculture. There are two possible interpretations to rates of return in Malthus' writings: One less known in which (unspecified) prices are related to cost of production, the other most commonly known, involving output and inputs.

Version 1. Return: Unspecified* **Cost:** Production.
The law stated: "…in every rich and improving country there is a natural and strong tendency to a constantly increasing price* of raw produce, owing to the necessity of employing, progressively, land of an inferior quality." (Winch: 69, citing Malthus 1815).

*__Note__: The return (e.g. net profit) is not specifically mentioned in the above passage; the logic suggests that the return is same-period profit, in that higher prices in that period can help maintain profits in the face of rising costs of production.

Version 2. Return: Output **Cost:** Unspecified --Inputs.
The *law of diminishing returns* (Malthus 1815) as it appears to be more commonly known relates the *quantity of inputs* and the *quantity of output* for productive processes (Stigler: 133); note that this formulation does not necessarily involve *costs*. As increasing increments of a particular input (for example, labor) are added, there comes a point that the resulting increments of output or "product" (i.e. marginal product) may *decline*.

While costs are omitted in the above formulation the field of *producer microeconomics* introduces costs, prices and production cost curves of the inputs and goods produced into the analysis so as to compute a *profit-maximizing* point. When graphically representing costs of production and profit maximization, typically the x-axis is the quantity Q of output, and the y-axis is the cost/price. Costs are generally assumed to be incurred at the approximately same time as the output. The concept of "returns to scale" can be mentioned here, which can be divided into *constant* or *variable* returns to scale (*variable* being either increasing or decreasing). (Stigler: 150-151) See the next section (prior period costs) for an example of constant returns to scale in a macro-economic context: The Cobb-Douglas production function (Cobb, Douglas 1928).

The Law of Accelerating Returns. (Kurzweil 2001). Ray Kurzweil in his seminal online essay states: "An analysis of the history of technology shows that technological change is exponential....(T)he "returns," such as chip speed and cost-effectiveness, also increase exponentially." Defining chip speed as a return can be viewed as a form of *output* which accelerates as the costs of producing the technologies may be expected to decline. In terms of rates of return for financial entities engaged in these technologies, while profound shifts may occur at some point after biological and non-biological intelligence merge the question remains whether the drive to economize will be any less prevalent.

Prior Period (Sunk) Costs

Prior period costs, or sunk costs, are those incurred prior to the period in which the return is generated, recorded on a *balance sheet*, whether at the firm or national level. It should be recalled that there may be a mix of *both* same period and prior period costs on the balance sheet; a portion of items on the balance sheet that represent costs incurred in the same period, such as *capital expenditures*. For example, if in fiscal year 2015 the net cash flow is compared to the assets of the firm, the assets as of the end of fiscal year 2015 include those that were added onto the balance sheet during fiscal year 2015. If the business has been operating for more than a year, the balance sheet also would also likely include assets acquired in prior periods (i.e. prior period costs of investment).

It should be noted that in the historical (and even modern) literature, the definition of "capital" or "stock" is not always entirely clear unless provided by the authors. There can be more than one meaning of "capital" in the same paragraph, such as capital in *capital expenditures/fixed assets* and *capital contributions* by equity investors. A best attempt is made to determine what the term means in financial and financial accounting.

Background Information. It may help to review the accounting identity of the balance sheet here:

$$\text{Total Assets*} = \text{Total Capital}$$

$$\text{Total Capital} = \text{Liabilities} + \text{Equity}$$

A generic balance sheet is shown here for reference:

BALANCE SHEET EXAMPLE

ASSETS	LIABILITIES
Cash, Equivalents & S-T Investments	Accounts Payable, Accrued Expenses
Accounts Receivable	S-T Loans, Credit Lines, Notes Payable
Inventories	Current Maturities L-T Debt (CPLTD)
P,P&E, Net (fixed assets)	**Long-Term Debt**
Business Assets (Equity Method) (1)	**EQUITY**
Other Investments (2)	Shareowners' Equity (3)
Intangible Assets (Trademarks/Goodwill)	Capital Surplus
Other Assets	Reinvested/Retained Earnings
	Treasury Stock, at cost
TOTAL ASSETS	**TOTAL CAPITAL (Liabilities + Equity)**

Notes
(1) Equity Investments with a controlling interest
(2) Includes non-controlling equity interests
(3) For example: Common Stock, par value, authorized and issued.
Long-term assets and liabilities are in bold face.
Abbreviations: Short-term= S-T, Long-Term=L-T

Referring back to the framework table, **Category #2A** is Assets of a Financial Entity which consist of the entity's *fixed assets* or can extend to its *total assets*.

Fixed Assets. A brief review of fixed assets is provided here. "Plant, property and equipment, net of accumulated depreciation" (PP&E, net) can also be referred to as "fixed capital" or "fixed assets." For example, this PP&E, net, is reported at cost on December 31, 2015 and represents an accumulation of purchases of items of PP&E in the past up to December 31, 2015. Note that some PP&E (such as an old tractor on a farm, or a printer in an office) may no longer be operational, but as long as they are still owned by the company, would form part of this "stock" of PP&E

assets of the company, reported at the original cost of the vehicle or machine on the balance sheet (but possibly worth zero even as scrap if the company attempted to dispose of it). The logic can be scaled up to an economy as many studies have done, to arrive at the "capital stock" of an economy.

Profitability Ratios

A type of *financial ratio* called the *profitability ratio* (Damodaran 79-86; Dorsey 85-90) is generally applicable to prior period (sunk) costs. The profitability ratio is a form of rate of return on a chosen measure of assets or capital of the firm. **Note:** Recall that the term "profitability" defined as *net profit/revenues* is not a rate of return measure.

The term "profitability" as a rate of return is relevant to prior period costs; the numerator is the *net profit* of the financial entity in a given time period (*net profit* is often abbreviated as "profit").

Assets: Category #2A. Common *profitability ratios* related to *assets* of a financial entity are the *return on assets* (ROA), the *return on fixed assets*, or variations:

ROA. Return on Assets (ROA) is expressed as the following:

ROA=Net Profit/Total Assets

A variation of ROA centered on *fixed assets* or *PP&E* is *return on fixed assets* (or "fixed capital"):

Net Profit/Fixed Assets

ROA at the Macro-Level

Scaling up to a macroeconomic level, similar exercises have been attempted to apply profitability ratios to national or regional economies; the fixed assets of firms may be renamed and redefined somewhat. Rates of return may be calculated as a ratio of some measure of profitability of firms/financial entities (or output) relative to the fixed assets of firms nationwide (also called "capital formation" or "gross fixed capital formation"). This type of analysis can be found for certain types of government projects, infrastructure spending (public investment), or public-private investment projects. Historical examples are provided further below.

Assets: Category #2A and #2B Clarifications

Additions to Assets within Category #2A. The rate of return most relevant for anticipated *additions* to assets (such as capital expenditures or business acquisitions) is covered in the section on Future Costs (forward-looking decisions).

Financial Entities in Category #2B. As ongoing financial entities, the rate of return on cost (RRC) is a measure of rate of return that applies to financial entities, even if owned as assets. This category is covered in the section on Future Costs for the scenario when the acquisition of a financial entity (business, income real estate) is being considered. Once the business is acquired, profitability ratios in addition to other measures of performance may be applied.

Capital as Assets to Investors: Category #3 and #4

The following profitability ratios may be of particular interest to investors in the company as measures of rates of return. Recall that this capital (debt capital, equity capital or both) is the capital of the financial entity that represents an asset to investors/owners. Category #3 applies if the asset generates current income, and category #4 for non-income generating assets.

The profitability ratios that refer to the "capital" side of the identity include *return on invested capital* (ROIC) or *return on capital* (ROC) and *return on equity* (ROE). Note that there can be a number of variations of these measures and only a few are presented here.

ROIC (or **ROC**) =NOPAT/ Invested Capital

…where NOPAT is net operating profit after taxes, and *invested capital* is defined as *total assets* less non-interest-bearing current liabilities such as accounts payable and other current assets and excess cash (cash not required for daily operations) (Dorsey 2004:95).

In a variation of the ROIC above, Hitchner (2011) relates NCF to overall invested capital and calls it *invested capital net cash flow*. The NCF variation on ROE is NCF to equity, or *equity net cash flows*. (648)

ROE or *Return on Equity* is net profit divided by the equity of the firm.

The return on investment (ROI) is the subject of the next section, and should be regarded as distinct from the profitability ratios above.

Note: Return *of* Capital. A point to clarify is the term "the return *of* capital" which uses the word "return," but in the context of *financing activity*. For example, when a lender loans money, it is expected that the loan be repaid with interest. The repayment is in the form of interest and principal; the "return" in this usage is simply the *repayment* of the principal/capital that was lent to the borrower, and does not itself represent a return, except in the sense of repayment. The same reasoning could apply to an investor who when selling an asset, hopes for the full return of his/her capital in addition to a capital gain. In this case, the return of capital is the amount of the original investment made.

Rate of Return on Investment (ROI)

The *rate of return on investment* (also abbreviated as the "return on investment" or ROI) includes both current income of the asset and any capital appreciation. The ROI should not be confused with the *return on invested capital* (ROIC), which is a *profitability ratio* introduced in the previous section.

A simple ROI can be calculated as follows:

(Gain on Asset + Current Income) / Cost of Asset

…where the *gain* is the difference between the purchase price and the selling price of the asset; of course the gain could also be a loss when the purchase price is greater than the selling price. The numerator also includes any income earned from the asset during the holding period, such as dividends/distributions or interest.

Applications of the ROI. With regards to financial entities, the ROI can apply to:
Category #2A-Assets of the financial entity;

Category #3 or #4 --investments in assets that are also the capital of the financial entity.

ROI can also apply to category #4 assets that are *unrelated* to financial entities, such as investments in commodities or collectibles (Category #4B).

Category #2A Assets. The ROI typically involves a prior-period cost so as to evaluate the historical performance of an asset. Firms may choose to calculate the historical ROI on individual assets held, and therefore is included in the framework table as a measure of rate of return. The variables are: Purchase price (acquisition cost) and the selling price (net of any costs related to the sale such as commissions).

For examples of decision-making about investments to be made in the future, see the section on Future Costs (forward-looking decisions); these methods may be more common than ROI for investment decisions to be made

Category #3 Asset ROI Single-Year Example. The stock of a company is purchased for 100 currency units that pays a dividend of 10 currency units per year. There is no capital appreciation of the asset in that year and at the end of a year the stock is sold for the same price as it was bought. In this case, the ROI would be:

$$(110-100)/100=0.10$$
*(to obtain the percentage 10% multiply 0.10 by 100)

Category #4B Asset ROI Single-Year Example. An antique is purchased for 100 currency units and one year later is sold for 150 currency units. The ROI on this asset (investment) would be:

$$(150-100)/100=0.50$$

Category #3 and #4A Combined ROI Single-Year Example. A bond of a company is purchased for 100 currency units that pays interest of 2 currency units per year. The bond is sold for 110 at the end of a year and therefore the capital appreciation of the bond in that year is 10 currency units. In this case, the ROI would be:

$$[(110-100) +2]/100=.12$$

Note that in this example the rate of return is a "hybrid" of both Category #3 and #4 because there is a portion of the return that comes from current income, and a portion that comes from future purchasing power (in this case capital appreciation).

Annual ROI Multi-Year Example (CAGR)
The previous examples were for ROIs over a single year. What if the returns are computed over many years? In this case, the compound annual growth rate (CAGR) is a common and handy tool to computing the annual ROI over more than one year of historical data.

Category #4B Asset: Gold. An investment in gold does not involve payment of cash dividends (and may involve storage costs). For example, if an investor had bought an ounce of gold at $300/ounce in 1999 then sold near the 2011 peak at $1750, and assuming no storage costs were incurred by the investor, the return as computed by the compound annual growth rate (CAGR) would be about 16% per year.

The formula for the CAGR can be constructed in spreadsheet programs. The steps are to divide the final selling price by the purchase price; the result is then raised to the power $1/n$ where n is the number of years between the two events (to obtain the correct number of years, count from the year *after the purchase*, and *include* the year of the sale). Then take the figure, which should be a ratio and subtract 1 from this figure, then multiply by 100. In the above gold investment, the asset was sold 12 years after purchase, so:

$$(1750/300)^{(1/12)}=1.158$$
$$(1.158-1) \times 100= 15.8\%$$

This CAGR figure for ROI can be compared to the IRR for the same scenario in the section on IRR Employing Historical Data with identical results.

38

Expected Return and ROI Measure (Link to Future Costs). For a measure of expected return using the ROI formula with expected payoffs and probabilities, see the section Future Costs, rates of return in valuation theory and expected return as E (NPV).

Financing, Cash Flow and Accounting Clarifications. Rates of return on Category #3 and #4 assets apply equally to both securities acquired in secondary markets or in new issues. However, from the firm perspective, purchases by investors of their equity or debt securities in secondary markets (of already-existing securities) are distinct from purchases of *new issues* of securities. In the case of secondary market purchases, the business financing and cash flow is unaffected.

In the case of new issuance and capital contributions or loans, while the entity receives cash *inflows* from the investors, these are strictly due to *financing activity* related to the entity's capital.

Profitability Ratios: Historical Examples

John Stuart Mill (1848) uses several examples of returns on the subject of the "tendency of profits to a minimum" in an early example of prior period costs. The capital could be defined as both capital contributed by investors, as well as the fixed assets that are built and/or purchased with investor capital:

"And much (new capital) is absolutely wasted. Mines are opened, railways or bridges made, and many other works of uncertain profit commenced, and in these enterprises much capital is sunk which yields either no return, or none adequate to the outlay." (98)

Here, the returns can refer to those of the (failed) enterprises, as in ROA but also to the returns for the investors in the projects as ROE.

ROA. Adam Smith (1776), in a rebuttal of Locke, Law and Montesquieu (316) on the subject of the "real cause of the lowering of the rate of interest through the greater part of Europe." (316) While they and others claimed that the increase in the quantity of precious metals (gold and silver) from the discovery in the Spanish West Indies resulted in lower interest rates, Smith explains his reasoning with *the profits of stock*,* or in current terminology, most likely a measure similar to ROA. "Any increase in the quantity of silver, while that of the commodities circulated by means of it remained the same could have no other effect than to diminish the value of that metal. The nominal value of all sorts of goods would be greater, but their real value would be precisely the same as before. ... *The profits of stock would be the same both nominally and really.* ...the profits of stock are not computed by the number of pieces of silver with which they are paid, *but by the proportion which those pieces bear to the whole capital employed.* Smith notes that "ten per cent" as the common profits of stock, and states that the "common proportion between capital and profit, therefore, would be the same, and consequently the common interest of money...." (318) (italics added for emphasis)

*According to Friedman, "profits of stock" as the return to *non-human, reproducible capital* (i.e. fixed assets) was progressively renamed to *interest* or *quasi-rent*, and the word *profits* came to refer to the earnings of management, with special reference to the reward for bearing uncertainty (Friedman, 1986: 279).

Note: A possible source of confusion is that Smith's "profits of stock" are actually the rate of return on fixed assets/assets but since *"rate of"* is not stated the "profit" could be mistakenly thought to be the absolute figure of profits.

ROA: Assets at Market Value. In an interesting variation on prior period costs, Ricardo relates the return (profits) to the *market value* of assets of the agricultural enterprise, revalued from their original cost. First, Ricardo (1821) in a financial accounting of farm activity begins with the "original capital"* of the farmer of 3000 *l.*, then calculating the profits of his *stock of capital* as declining from 16 per cent to 14.8 per cent as the price per quarter of wheat rises. (117) Ricardo then remarks that the *rate* of profits will fall even further, because of the value of the capital* of the farmer that would "all rise in price in consequence of the rise of produce." (117)

*The "capital" referred to here is not the original capital contribution (as in financing activity) but the capital embodied in the farm as *assets* (acquired in a prior as well as in the same period). He gives examples of such assets as "...raw produce, such as his corn and hay-ricks, his unthreshed wheat and barley, his horses and cows..." Therefore he is computing a rate of return on

40

assets of the farm, as measured by the return on assets (ROA) or profits/assets.

Ricardo points out that the decline in the rate of return on assets causes a disincentive for other possible entrepreneurs to invest in such economic activity, as the venture is relatively less profitable. As noted above, although the original capital was 3000 *l*., after a rise in prices Ricardo states,

"...the value of the farmer's stock would be greatly increased from its necessarily consisting of many of the commodities which had risen in value...." (122). "If then his profit were 180 *l*., or 6 per cent on his original capital, profits would not at that time be really at a higher *rate* than 3 per cent.; for 6000 *l*. at 3 percent gives 180 *l*.; and on those terms only could a new farmer with 6000*l*. money in his pocket enter into the farming business." (Ricardo 122)

In sum, due to the rising market value of assets, the rate of profit declines from 6 percent or 180/3000 to 3 percent: 180/6000.

Macro-Level Rates of Return on Assets (ROA)

A few historical examples of country-level analysis of rates of return are provided here.

Net Profit to Capital Stock. Scott (1988) looks at the average rate of return as the *net profit (before tax) / net capital stock* for various countries. The net profits are equal to gross trading profits – depreciation at current replacement cost – stock appreciation. The net capital stock is at current replacement cost less accumulated depreciation and includes inventories and land.

Estimating rates of return for the nonfinancial corporate sector, the average postwar real rates of return in UK and USA are estimated at .089 (1951-73), and .114 (1948-73), respectively (exponential rates per annum). (207)

Income (All Forms) to Fixed Capital (Firm and National level) Piketty (2014) analyzes rates of return at both the firm and national level. He defines return as the "...yield on capital over the course of a year regardless of its legal form (profits, rents, dividends, interest, royalties, capital gain*, etc.)...." (52) *Capital* as defined by Piketty is likely a balance sheet classification similar to Plant, Property and Equipment (PP&E) or "fixed capital." In an example using both the return and the capital for a firm, Piketty states: "....a firm that uses capital valued* at 5 million euros (including offices, infrastructure, machinery, etc.), to produce 1 million euros worth of goods annually, with 600,000 euros going to pay workers and 400,000 euros in profits." In the example, the rate of return on capital would then be 400,000/5,000,000 or 8 percent. (54)

*Notes. The value of the P, P&E is not clarified, but would likely be reported at cost. Note that capital gains are included in Piketty's measure of return.

A critical distinction between capital gain and current income is discussed elsewhere here and by Fisher as cited previously (1930:25).

In order to avoid the possibility of double-counting of income, if profits are undistributed then dividends should not be added; firm profits should be net of interest and royalty income.

Output (Total Product) as a Form of Return

Output is a special form of return which is very roughly reviewed here. In the literature on *diminishing returns* discussed previously, output can be represented in graphical form relative to the input needed to produce the output, where the x-axis shows the input (such as labor, fuel, or quantity Q of some other input), and the y-axis shows the output (such as power generation, total product, etc.). However, the costs of the input(s) are not necessarily known from this representation, nor the profitability.

Return: Total Production **Cost (prior period)**: Fixed Assets. In the celebrated *Cobb-Douglas production function*, returns to scale are constant, the return is output defined as total production, and the inputs are *capital* and *labor*. The *capital*, which refers to the real value of plant, property and equipment, could be viewed as a prior period cost (and partly same period cost as the capital stock may include fixed capital added in the same period as the return). Labor as an input is represented by person-hours worked per year, not cost in terms of wages. (Cobb, Douglas 1928).

Note: Macro Models and Public Investment Policy. In the 20th century, production functions and models linking fixed capital as an input to national output may have provided a rationale for public policy to increase investment--whether public or stimulation of private investment--to spur development. A number of economists have studied the record of such investment in the 20th century and a summary of their findings are noted in the Appendices.

Internal Rate of Return (IRR) in Prior Period Costs. The internal rate of return is detailed below in the section on future costs because the literature on capital budgeting tends to emphasize the IRR in the context of decision-making for future investments. However, it is possible for the IRR to involve prior period costs --when the data is *historical* and the initial outlay was made in the past. In the next section the case of the IRR applied to historical financial data of a firm is explored.

FUTURE COSTS (FORWARD-LOOKING DECISIONS)

Introduction. Future costs involve *decision-making* about whether to make an asset purchase; the assets of Category #2 through #4 of the framework table all can apply. Examples include (#2A) additions to fixed assets (equipment) as a *capital expenditure* or *(#2B) acquisition of a business or technology embodied in a business process* which represent cash *outflows* from the financial entity. The analysis of *valuation* of assets may also be categorized into future costs because decisions are to be made about a particular cost to be incurred. The decision maker can be a representative of a business or other organization (#1A), or an individual (Category #1B) such as a homeowner considering installation of a solar heating unit on the roof. This section covers elements of the subject of *discounted cash flow* (DCF) analysis and *capital budgeting*. Because the subject of DCF analysis deserves a book of its own, summary main points will be covered as best as possible, while mixing in historical references to highlight the evolution and differences in approach to rates of return.

Rate of Return Measures. There are basically three types of rate of return measure in connection with future costs. These three rates of return may also be referred to as a *discount rate* because the discount rate is the rate at which a future stream of income (usually net cash flows) is *discounted* to the present to arrive at a measure of *present value* (PV). The discount rate and rate of return are treated synonymously here and will occasionally be joined together as *rate of return/discount rate*.

1. The Internal Rate of Return (IRR)
2. Financing Cost (as estimated by various methods)
3. Capitalization Rates

Iteration. In the case of the #1, the IRR, the rate of return/discount rate is the result of an *iterative process* in which the present value (PV) is equated to the initial cost outlay so that NPV=0, as will be shown later.

Estimation and Valuation Theory. Financing cost (#2) and capitalization rates (#3) generally relate to *valuation theory* and the *valuation of assets* in which a *present value* (PV) of the asset is computed. (Damodaran 1996, 2012). Both of these rates of return are the result of some form of *estimation process* relying on certain underlying variables. During the 20th century, the estimation approach for capitalization rates has become similar to that of Measure #2 *financing cost*.

Risk and Uncertainty. A critical extension of the analysis of rate of return is accounting for *uncertainty* and *risk*, which will be touched upon further below.

Rate of Return Measure #1: Internal Rate of Return (IRR).

The *internal rate of return* (IRR) is a common measure of rate of return applicable to decision-making about future asset purchases; refer to the Framework table for the categories to which the IRR can apply. The IRR is computed by *iteration*, with the first period a *negative* cash outflow followed by a series of positive net cash inflows (i.e. the flows of the cost and the net benefit are directionally opposite). This first period cash outflow corresponds to a purchase price, cost incurred or cash outlay. Even if the future stream of net cash flows is known, the IRR cannot be computed until a figure for an initial outlay (as a negative) can be supplied. Therefore the order of decision-making is PP→IRR where information about the purchase price (PP) or initial outlay typically precedes the calculation of the IRR.

It should be noted that many financial entities (businesses) have a *required* or *hurdle rate of return*. Therefore, decision-makers may have a reasonable idea of where the purchase price should be in order to meet the desired rate of return target.

Methodology. The IRR is a method of computing a rate of return which is based on *iteration* of future anticipated stream of benefits; most commonly this stream of benefits refers to *net cash flows* generated by an asset. The internal rate of return (IRR) equates the present value (PV) of a series of such future benefits to the *initial outlay* (or investment cost), according to the following procedure, starting with the present value (PV):

$$PV = NCF_1/(1+r) + NCF_2/(1+r^2)+...+NCF_n/(1+r^n)$$

Where NCF is the future *net cash flow*, and r is the rate of return/discount rate. When the amount of the initial cost outlay is deducted from the present value the *net present value* (NPV) is obtained. Recall that this *initial cost outlay* (IC) is incurred at the beginning of the period of cash flows.

$$NPV = PV - IC$$

To obtain the IRR, the NPV is set to zero, or NPV=0, or PV- IC=0; Now, r becomes the *internal rate of return* (IRR):

$$NCF_1/(1+r) + NCF_2/(1+r^2)+...+NCF_n/(1+r^n)- IC = 0$$

Note that future *net* cash flows are often abbreviated as "cash flows."

Future Benefits. It is typical for the IRR to be computed on the basis of a *future stream of cash flows*. It is often overlooked that the IRR can also be computed based on *future savings* (another form of expressing a future stream of net cash flows), as well as *future purchasing power* of the particular asset (including cash/currency).

Risk and Uncertainty Factor. The question of risk and probable cash flows is also critical to the analysis, and when introduced, changes the designation of future net benefits to *expected* future net benefits (e.g. *expected* future net cash flows).

Applications of the IRR

Bond Yield (YTM) as Rate of Return. In bond valuation analysis the IRR is referred to as a *yield to maturity* (YTM), representing a rate of return to the bond investor. (Damodaran: 398) This rate of return is also referred to as the "yield" and includes both the "coupon" (interest payment) and any capital appreciation of the bond. It should be added that the discount rate will "vary from bond to bond, depending upon default risk, with higher rates used for riskier bonds and lower rates for safer ones." (398)

Historical Note. The IRR/yield to maturity is also referred to as an "interest rate" of the bond, which may give rise to some potential confusion in the historical analysis and definition of interest rates, a detailed in the Appendix.

Decision-Making with IRR: Rate-of-Return Rule. The IRR can be applied to a simple decision-making rule called the *rate-of-return rule* (Brealey and Myers: 14). If the calculated rate of return (e.g. IRR) of a particular asset exceeds, or equals a comparable alternative asset, then the asset purchase (aka "investment") can be accepted, with certain exceptions noted in the literature. This rule can be referred to as the "rate-of-return" rule and can be shown as follows:

$$r_1 \geq r_2$$

Where r_1 is the calculated rate of return for the particular asset under study, and r_2 is the rate of return of an alternative asset*. For example, if the rate of return for r_1 is calculated to be 10%, and the rate of return on an alternative comparable asset r_2 is 9%, then r_1, the particular asset being evaluated would theoretically be a good candidate for purchase. Note that these percentage figures normally would be expected to be per annum, and cover the same time period.

*Note that the rate of return of the alternative asset is often referred to as a "cost" or "opportunity cost of capital" of the first asset; the rate of return for the alternative asset could also be the *minimum required rate of return* of an investor). Opportunity cost is what is *lost* by taking a particular course of action.

Rates of Return Comparisons with the IRR: Examples

The IRR is computed for pairs of assets (*a* and *b*) in three possible scenarios in order to decide between alternative assets employing the "rate-of-return rule":

Scenario 1: Asset generates a future stream of net cash flow

Scenario 2: Asset generates a future stream of net cash flow from savings (reduction of expenses);

Scenario 3: Asset produces no future stream of net cash flows but has *greater or lesser purchasing power* at the end of a given term;

It should be clarified that the 3rd case, increased purchasing power, involves two possible scenarios, *asset appreciation* and *deflation*.

1. **Deflation/Inflation (Cash and Equivalent)**. Increased purchasing power due to *deflation*, in which the ability of cash, currency and equivalent assets which have monetary characteristics to purchase more of the same goods and services than previously. (Note*)

2. **Asset Appreciation**. Increased purchasing power due to appreciation of the particular asset relative to cash/currency. For example, the purchase of a Pokémon™ card that increases in value over time and is sold for more currency units than were paid out to acquire the asset.

Although in deflation cash may effectively "appreciate" in that more goods and services can be bought with the same amount of cash as before, it is not common to call an increase in the purchasing power of cash "asset appreciation."

It also should be recognized that computing a rate of return for non-cashflow-producing assets such as cash in a deflationary or inflationary scenario may not be viewed as conventional.

*Note: Precious metals such as gold have historically had monetary characteristics even though our current (early 21st century) monetary system does not view gold as currency. In an inflationary environment in which fiat currencies are being debased it is theoretically possible for monetary-type assets to appreciate in value against the depreciating cash/currency as well as to benefit from greater purchasing power in a deflationary environment.

No adjustments for risk of loss or probabilities of cash flows are being made here, although these should also factor into the decision-making process.

TABLE: COMPARISON OF SCENARIOS (IRR)

Scenarios and Asset Pair Comparisons	Future Cash Flow		Future Savings		Future Purchasing Power	
	Asset 1a	Asset 1b	Asset 2a	Asset 2b	Asset 3a	Asset 3b
Initial Outlay	-1	-1.2	-1	-1.1	-1	-1
Periodic Net Benefits	0.1	0.115	0.1	0.11	n/a	n/a
Periods (Years)	30	30	12	12	7	7
Net Benefit at Term	1	1	0	0	1.25	0.93

The table above shows pairs of assets in the three basic scenarios and the data is provided for purposes of illustration.

Future Net Cash Flow Stream. The first scenario, titled "Future Net Cash Flow" begins with column 1 (Asset 1a) , in which an investor buys a bond for 1 currency unit that pays $1/10^{th}$ of that amount (or 0.10 currency unit) to the investor every year for 30 years. A competing asset (Asset 1b) is more expensive to purchase (1.2 currency units) but pays a slightly higher periodic net benefit of 0.11 over the same period of time. In both cases, at the end of the 30 years the investor receives his/her principal (the original amount paid in). The IRR for 1a and 1b are 10% and 9%, respectively (figures rounded). According to the rate-of-return rule, in theory, 1a would be the preferable investment.

Future Savings Stream (Variation on Future Net Cash Flow). This second scenario is a variation on the above scenario since it too involves a future stream of cash flows, but in the form of savings. A homeowner is given the option of two solar power systems, each which are expected to yield savings over the homeowner's future energy bills. The solar power system that generates the savings (additional future cash flow from reduced energy expenses) is an asset. Asset 2b is 10% more expensive that Asset 2a, but generates more savings as seen in the table. However, the system is only expected to have a usable "life" of about 12 years, and after that, there is no return of the original amount paid other than perhaps the scrap value of the copper tubing – we assume a net benefit of zero at the end of the 12 years. In this comparison, although Asset 2b generates higher savings, over 12 years the IRR is still higher for Asset 2a (5%) versus Asset 2b (3%), and by the rate-of-return rule, Asset 2a is the preferred alternative. (Note that if the usable life is extended to 30 years, Asset 2a still leads at 11% versus Asset 2b at 9%).

Future Purchasing Power

The third scenario concerns assets that generate no future stream of net cash flow but which have greater purchasing power at the end of a given term. This third scenario can be divided into two sub-scenarios: The first involving cash/equivalent; the second involving appreciation of other assets.

Deflation/Inflation Case (Cash and Equivalent). In scenario 3, a saver puts aside 1 currency unit for the future (the "asset" is the cash or currency saved). Two cases are explored, deflation and inflation; the asset is cash in both cases but the deflation case is labelled Asset 3a, and the inflation case is labelled Asset 3b.

Deflation (3a). Over a 7-year period deflation has resulted in the same 1 currency unit being able to purchase 25% more goods and services than before. The "net benefit" of 0.25 is due to the deflation which increased the purchasing power of the currency over the time period, plus the original 1 currency unit is "returned" to the saver. The theoretical IRR of the cash is computed at 3%.

Inflation (3b). Asset 3b undergoes a sustained period of *inflation* (i.e. reduced purchasing power), and at the end of 7 years the cash only can purchase 93% of what could be purchased previously; in this inflation case, the IRR is *negative* 1%; this can be interpreted as a decline in purchasing power of 1% per year over the period.

It should be noted that forecasting consumer price deflation or deflation may be a difficult task. Although inflation (even at low levels) is a common feature of many modern economies, there is an argument for keeping a certain amount of liquid assets at hand to take advantage of the possibility of declining prices, whether consumer or asset prices.

Asset Appreciation Case. The same scenario #3 and data can also describe *asset appreciation*, as in the example noted above where an investor decides to invest in a Pokémon™ card (Asset 3a) and a Yugio™ card (Asset 3b) both that pay no stream of cash flows. Suppose that Asset 3a (the Pokémon™ card) is able to command more cash than before due to future favorable market conditions than Asset 3b, the Yugio™ card which turned out to be less popular and in fact lost money. Asset 3a would be the better investment. Someone knowledgeable of the market for such cards might be able to gauge future market trends to capitalize upon such opportunities.

IRR in Historical Reference

In the early literature on *discounted cash flow analysis* and *capitalization theory*, Frank Fetter (1914) clarified the importance of the rate of discount (rate of return) as embodying both interest and profit expectations. He uses the terms "rates of profit", "value-surplus" and "net surplus" and defines productivity as "…the capacity which goods bought with judgment at current prices, have, in the hands of enterprisers, of yielding *a net surplus, sufficient not only to remunerate them, but to pay contract interest to lenders….*" "The amount of interest which enterprisers estimate they can afford to pay…is the difference between the discounted, or present, worth of products imputable to these agents and their worth at the time they are expected to mature. The prices of the agents, which are the costs, involve (not presuppose) a rate of discount." (1914: 86-98) (Italics added)

Rate of Return over Cost. Irving Fisher's *rate of return over cost* and Keynes' *marginal efficiency of capital* both describe discounting and the comparison of alternative streams of income in the context of investment analysis and rates of return on investment. (Backhouse: 157, Keynes 1936, Fisher 1930, Solow 1963). For any single stream of income, this rate of return can be referred to as the *internal rate of return* (IRR), to be detailed elsewhere.

The *rate of return over cost* refers to the return as the equalizing rate when comparing the present value (present worth) of two alternative income streams. With his exposition of the *method of comparative advantage* Fisher combines both the *internal rate of return* (of each income stream individually) and *opportunity cost* (when comparing the two separate income streams), although he may not have used those terms: "This hypothetical rate of interest which if used in calculating the present worth of the two options compared would equalize them or their differences (cost and return) may be called the rate of return over cost and hereafter this name will generally be employed." [Fisher 1930 as cited in Econ Library (II.VII.16)]

Growth in Return and Rates of Return. Harold Hotelling (1931) conducted landmark research in the economics of exhaustible resources; the *Hotelling principle* relates the *growth** in *net profit* to the *interest rate* (Devajaran 1981; Miller and Upton 1985). The equation is:

$$p_t = p_0 e^{rt}$$

Where the net profit is price minus cost, or more specifically "...the real price, net of marginal extraction costs." In more detail, p_t is "...interpreted as the net price received after paying the cost of extraction and placing upon the market, p_0 is the price in the initial period, and r is the rate of interest. Hotelling (1931:141). This equation could be reworded as "net profit grows at the rate of interest." Miller and Upton (1985) conduct an empirical test of the Hotelling valuation principle for the U.S. oil and gas industry.

In the Hotelling context the *rate of growth* in the net profit could be considered a rising future stream of benefits as in discounted cash flow (DCF) analysis. What is called the "interest rate" might be renamed the *internal rate of return* (IRR) as a discount rate from a future price p_t back to the present p_0 (where the PV is equal to the original price) As will be explained later in the concept of "future costs" the discount rate and rate of return are considered synonymous, and also can be derived by computation of the *internal rate of return* (IRR).

The Hotelling principle also may apply to other sectors of the economy: "...natural resources should be exploited at rates that tend to *equalize the rates of return on all assets together*, both exhaustible and other assets, mainly those traded regularly in financial and commodity markets (Klein: 124). (Italics added)

51

IRR Employing Historical Data: Exercises.

The internal rate of return is often used in conjunction with projections of *future* cash flows. However it is possible to compute the IRR with historical data to evaluate past performance –i.e. the past rate of return of a particular asset as measured by the IRR. Interestingly, a link is found between the multi-year return on investment (ROI) discussed above and the IRR.

Category #4B Asset Example: Precious Metals. As explained above, Category #4 assets generate no income/net cash flow for investors. Revisiting the example from the multi-year return on investment (ROI), if an investor had bought an ounce of gold at $300/ounce in 1999 then sold near the 2011 peak at $1750, and assuming no storage costs were incurred, the annual return as computed by the internal rate of return (IRR) would be about 16% per year. Recall that the compound annual growth rate (CAGR) in calculating a multi-year return on investment or ROI yielded the same result of 16% per annum.

Note that the rate of return can be highly sensitive to the acquisition date and sale date. Using a different set of dates such as purchase of an ounce near the 1979 peak and sale in 1999 the approximate IRR would have been roughly *negative* 5% per year.

The point here is not to cast a negative light on gold. Rather, having some understanding of asset markets and bubbles can aid in mitigating losses. Because severe asset overvaluation is typically followed by *collapses* in the prices of the assets, even quality assets acquired at or near a peak may require many years to return to the (inflated) purchase price following a collapse. The subject of asset mispricing and overvaluation is discussed at length below and is detailed extensively in Part II of this book.

Distinction between Nominal and Real Appreciation. As in the example above an asset appreciating at 16% per year is *nominal appreciation.* Nominal appreciation should be compared to measures of the *inflation rate* during the same period. For example, if the consumer price inflation rate had been 16% as well, the asset would have not appreciated at all in *real terms*: 16% nominal return– 16% inflation rate= 0% real return. A general goal of investing is for the purchasing power of investment to exceed the inflation rate.

Note that this example corresponds to **Scenario #3**: **Future Purchasing Power** in the IRR scenarios section above. The distinction is that the IRR in this example is being computed based on *historical data* for gold.

Category 1A#: Financial Entity (Firm): IRR with Historical Data. For the ongoing operations of a financial entity such as a firm, can an internal rate of return reasonably be computed? While it is computationally possible, for an ongoing business enterprise a number of questions are raised: (1) It is unclear which year should be the starting point for the initial cost outlays (2) if a starting point can be decided upon, it is unclear whether the business costs of production in that year can appropriately be treated as the initial cost outlay (3) does this initial cost outlay appropriately match the stream of net cash flows of the business in subsequent years; and (4) if so, how many years of net cash flows would be appropriate.

Despite these possible objections, for reference purposes the IRR was calculated based on historical data of an international consumer goods firm. The year of the first initial cash outlay (year 1) was arbitrarily decided upon; "years" refer to *fiscal* years. The initial cash outlay itself was assumed to be the firm's total cost of production in that fiscal year (defined as *Revenues less NNCF*), and the subsequent stream of net cash flows (defined as *NNCF*) was computed for 10 year rolling periods. This approach produces a set of separate IRR values for each fiscal year of the company, each with an initial cash outlay and its own 10 year stream of subsequent net cash flows. These IRR values are then compared with the net profit percentage (net profit/revenues) and the rate of return on cost (RRC); the RRC is a measure to be detailed in Part II along with the definition of NNCF.

Note: A 7-year periods IRR was also computed and a significant difference between the 7-year and 10-year average for the IRRs was observed. The average for the 7-year was 5%, some 8 percentage points lower than the 10-year periods IRR result of 13%; the 7-year standard deviation was one percentage point higher at 8%. It was decided that a longer time period would provide a better measure of the IRR. (The observation period was 1988 to 2004 for which a complete actual historical dataset was available for both the 7 and 10-year periods computations).

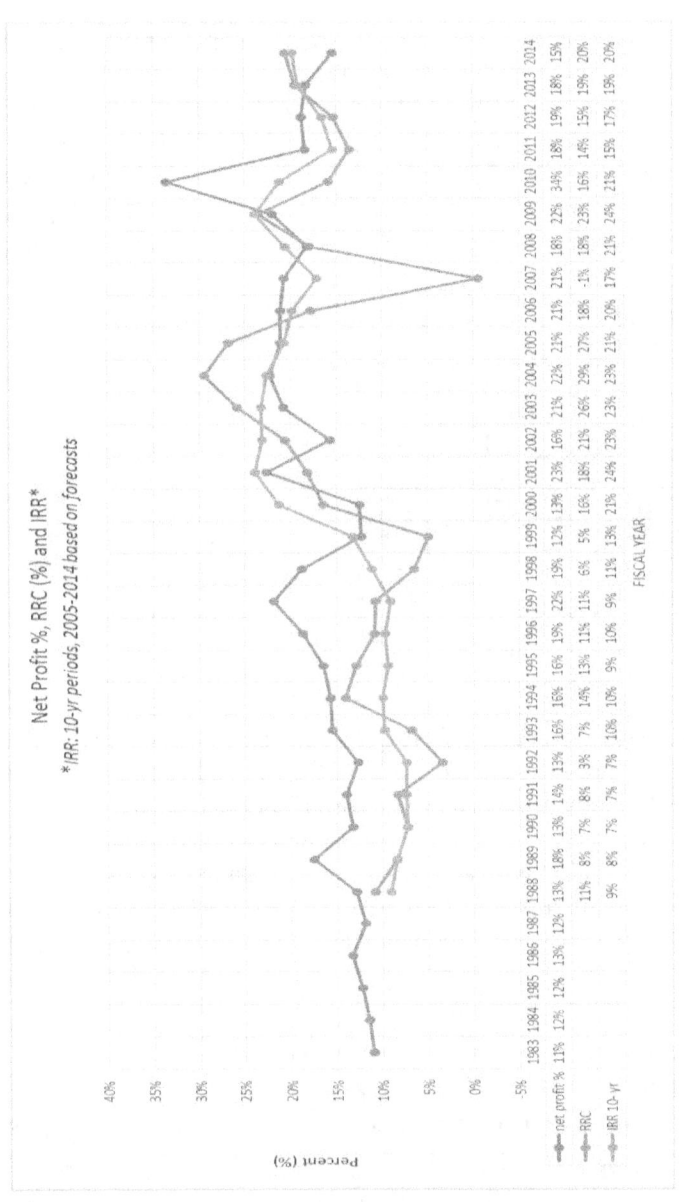

Net Profit %, RRC (%) and IRR*

*IRR: 10-yr periods, 2005-2014 based on forecasts

IRR Computations. For instance, each column below represents a single stream of cash flows beginning with the initial cash outflow at the top of the column (a negative figure, fiscal year

54

1988), followed by 10 years of subsequent net cash flows (positive figures). In the image below, the left column begins in 1988, and ends in 1998 at bottom. The top cell in the middle column is the initial cash outflow in 1989, followed by the net cash flows to 1999. This continues until the last year for which there is actual historical data (in this case 2004). The IRR stops at this point unless a forecast is constructed to add "future" missing data.

-7272		
673	-7949	
691	691	-9545
893	893	893
432	432	432
892	892	892
1994	1994	1994
2053	2053	2053
1828	1828	1828
1840	1840	1840
1142	1142	1142
	938	938
		2455

Results with Descriptive Statistics. The table below presents the results of three measures, the net profit percentage, the RRC and the IRR for comparison purposes. Note that there are *two* versions of the IRR, one to 2004 with the historical dataset complete, the other labelled (F)* with a *forecast* for the data needed for the IRR computation but missing after 2004. The forecast was constructed by applying the 10-year compound annual growth rate (CAGR) of the last 10 years of *actual* data of each variable* to the future years for which there was no data available yet.

(*the *initial cash outlays* and *subsequent annual net cash flows* were approximately 8.5% and 4.7%, respectively)

TABLE: IRR WITH HISTORICAL DATA AND COMPARISONS

COMPARISONS	NP %	NP%	RRC	IRR (F)	IRR
Mean	17.2%	18.2%	14.3%	15.6%	13.3%
Standard Deviation	4.7%	4.5%	7.5%	6.1%	6.5%
Observation Period	83-2014	88-2014	88-2014	88-2014	88-2004
Notes	*NP%=net profit/revenues			*(F)=forecast	

From this simple comparison, the mean (average) of both the IRR and the RRC may tend to be lower and more volatile that the net profit measure.

Shortcomings. The results suggest that the IRR could possibly be employed as a *comparative* rate of return measure with RRC and net profit percentages, but with significant limitations: First, despite the need for an extensive amount of historical data to conduct such an analysis, IRR calculations based on historical data are no longer possible after a certain point, requiring forecasts to bring the rate of return measures to the most current year.

Rates of Return in Valuation Theory

In valuation analysis, rate of return or *discount rate* is generally obtained by a process of *estimation*. Then, in a method called discounted cash flow (DCF) analysis this estimated rate is then used to discount future net cash flows to the present that are generated by a particular asset. The *present value* (PV) is the result.

The Return: NPV. Beginning with the *present value* (PV), the initial cost outlay (IC) (i.e. purchase price of the asset or investment) is deducted to arrive at the *net present value* (NPV) as follows:

$$NPV=PV-IC$$

In discounted cash flow (DCF) analysis this NPV could be described as the *return* or "net benefit" the investor hopes to generate in exchange for the cost outlay (purchase price); this is distinct from the rate of return itself, which is the discount rate.

A general process for decision-making among alternative investment opportunities from a valuation perspective (PV and NPV) is summarized as follows:

1. **Estimation of the rate of return/discount rate**. There are numerous methods to estimate discount rates and the literature is vast; the variables used in this process of estimation are based on various factors. The estimation of rate of return measure #2, *financing cost,* is detailed below.
2. **Factoring in Uncertainty.**

3. The Net Present Value (NPV) Rule.

Rate of Return Measure #2: Estimating Financing Cost. Above we studied the first rate of return measure, the *internal rate of return* (IRR). In valuation theory, it is more common to see the term "cost of capital", rather than rate of return. This *cost of capital* can be seen as a *financing cost* to the firm and is expressed typically as a percentage (per annum): This financing cost should be *weighted* since there is often a debt-equity mix involved. A measure of rate of return estimated is the *weighted average cost of capital* (WACC). It is important to note that this financing cost to the firm constitutes a *rate of return* to investors in the equity or debt financing, but does not represent the firm's own rate of return as a financial entity which is not addressed in this type of rate of return estimation.

The *weighted average cost of capital* incorporates the cost of both debt and equity financing for the firm, and once estimated can be used as the *discount rate* used in firm valuation. This financing cost can be expressed as $r_f = r_{fe}(e/(e+d)) + r_{fd}*(d/(e+d))$, where the overall financing cost is r_f; for equity this financing cost is r_{fe}, for debt it is r_{fd}. The market value of equity and debt are e and d and their proportions in the overall funding mix are represented by $(e/(e+d))$ and $(d/(e+d))$, respectively. The cost of debt is *after tax* and debt includes *convertible debt*. Preferred stock is ignored.

Scenarios. A **base scenario** assumes that the proportion of market values of equity and debt are 2/3 and 1/3, respectively, r_{fe} is 10% and r_{fd} is 5%: Financing cost for the firm as measured by the weighted average cost of capital is about 8.3%. **Scenario 2** assumes that the cost of equity remains at 10% and the after tax cost of debt now declines to 1%: Overall financing cost r_f now declines to 7%. **Scenario 3**, assuming a lowering of the cost of equity to 5%, and a decline in yields (interest rates) to 1%, r_f now declines to 3.7%. Note that over time, due to the cost differentials between equity and debt it is not impossible for firms to progressively shift their funding mix towards the cheaper source of financing, thereby further lowering the financing cost for firms. Just one example to illustrate this: Over time a firm's funding mix has shifted so that the proportion of equity and debt are now reversed: 1/3 and 2/3, respectively. Using the inputs from the last scenario above, the overall financing cost is now about 2.3%.

Interest Rate and Debt Maturity. Note that the interest rate used in the calculation of the cost of capital should be that of a debt instrument with a *maturity* (e.g. short-term, long-term) that closely matches the forecasted time period of the anticipated future income stream from the asset.

Estimating the Cost of Capital: Equity Portion. Examples of models that have been used to estimate the financing cost for the *equity* portion of the capital (r_{fe}) are briefly introduced below.

Models Overview. The *Capital Asset Pricing Model* (CAPM) (Markowitz 1952) assumes that expected returns of an asset are related to the market as a whole ("market portfolio").

$$E(R_i) = R_f + \beta([R_m] - R_f)$$

…where $E(R_i)$ is the *expected return on asset i*, R_f is the *riskfree* rate, and R_m is the expected return on *market portfolio*. Coefficient β is called the *beta* of asset *i*. A beta of 1.0 suggest that the asset (stock) moves in tandem with the market as a whole. The *risk premium on the market portfolio* ($[R_m] - R_f$ is the difference between the expected return on the market portfolio and the *riskfree* rate such as the yield on short-term government debt such as 90-day Treasury bills. The model is intimately connected with the concept of *risk*: For example, a stock with a beta of 1 moves so closely with the market that in an overall market downturn or crash such risk cannot be offset by diversification – this is called *systematic* or *nondiversifiable* risk.

Examples. A given firm's stock moves in tandem with the overall market so its beta is 1. The Treasury bill rate is 1% and the market premium is assumed to be 5%. The cost of equity (r_{fe}) is estimated at 6% or 1%+(1x5%). For a so-called "low beta" stock of 0.5, the cost of equity declines to 3.5%.

The *Arbitrage Pricing Model* (Ross 1976) features unanticipated risk originating from *firm-specific* and *marketwide* factors, the latter based on unanticipated changes in multiple economic variables. The *Multifactor Model* places further emphasis on macroeconomic variables (e.g. industrial production, GDP, changes in the term structure of interest rates) as well as financial metrics (e.g. price/book value ratios and market capitalization of firms).

Cost of Capital: Debt Portion. The cost of the *debt* is typically a function of interest rates, the firm's risk of default, and any tax benefits (Damodaran: 38, 63).

Decision-Making in Valuation Analysis

In this step, the investor must decide whether the asset purchase (investment) is worth making or not. In valuation theory, the NPV rule can apply, as explained below.

Net Present Value (NPV) Rule. The net present value (NPV) rule (Brealey and Myers: 14) can be applied to decision-making about the asset. The *cost of capital* (WACC) is estimated as noted above and serves as the discount rate in the calculation of the *present value* (PV) of a firm. A general formula for the PV of a *firm* with net cash flows (NCF) in perpetuity is shown here, where r represents this overall rate of return/discount rate which recall is a *financing cost*:

$$PV_f = \sum_{t=1}^{t=\infty} NCFt/(1+r)^t$$

Then, in an exercise potentially applicable to *mergers and acquisitions* (M&A) activity, this present value of the firm as calculated can then be compared to its potential acquisition cost in the market (i.e. the market value of the equities). In theory, if the calculated present value (PV) were to exceed the acquisition cost, then the target may be a good candidate for acquisition: PV>Cost.

The NPV rule states that investments with positive *net present values* (NPVs) should in theory be accepted; the net present values of various firms can be compared for possible acquisition (with adjustments made for risk, to be briefly noted below).

Note: Valuing Equity Alone. In order to value the *equity* of the firm rather than the firm itself, the market value of the firm's outstanding debt can be deducted. (Damodaran: 242)

When introducing the element of uncertainty, the stream of future cash flows to be discounted are *probable* future cash flows, detailed below in *risk and uncertainty*.

Rates of Return and Valuation Analysis: Other Considerations

Two factors to consider in valuation analysis are discussed below, policy interest rates, as well as adjusting for the uncertainty of future cash flows.

Policy Interest Rates and the Riskfree Rate: Historical Note

Policy interest rates (abbreviated as "policy rates") as they are referred to here and in Kennedy (2015) are official rates of interest set by monetary authorities in countries or jurisdictions which have a central bank. An example is the Federal Funds Rate in the United States, and more recently the interest rate on *excess reserves* of the banking system, which if lowered sufficiently could provide an impetus for massive lending by the banking system.

The *riskfree rate*, mentioned above in the context of valuation analysis and estimation of the discount rate may also be influenced by monetary policy. (Recall that the "interest rate" on bonds is more correctly referred to as a *yield* which includes the "rate" of the *riskfree* rate).

It is recognized that at various points in history, policy interest rates may not always have a uniform impact on lending behavior, but generally speaking policy interest rates can set a standard and a signal to the capital markets as to borrowing/financing costs; importantly, this includes loan rates in banking and yields on government debt (financing for government entities).

Secular Trend of Decline in Yields. We begin with the chart below showing the secular trend of policy interest rates in the U.S. as approximately represented by the *riskfree rate*, which can be referred to as the market yield on U.S. Treasury securities at 3-month constant maturity (quoted on investment basis). .

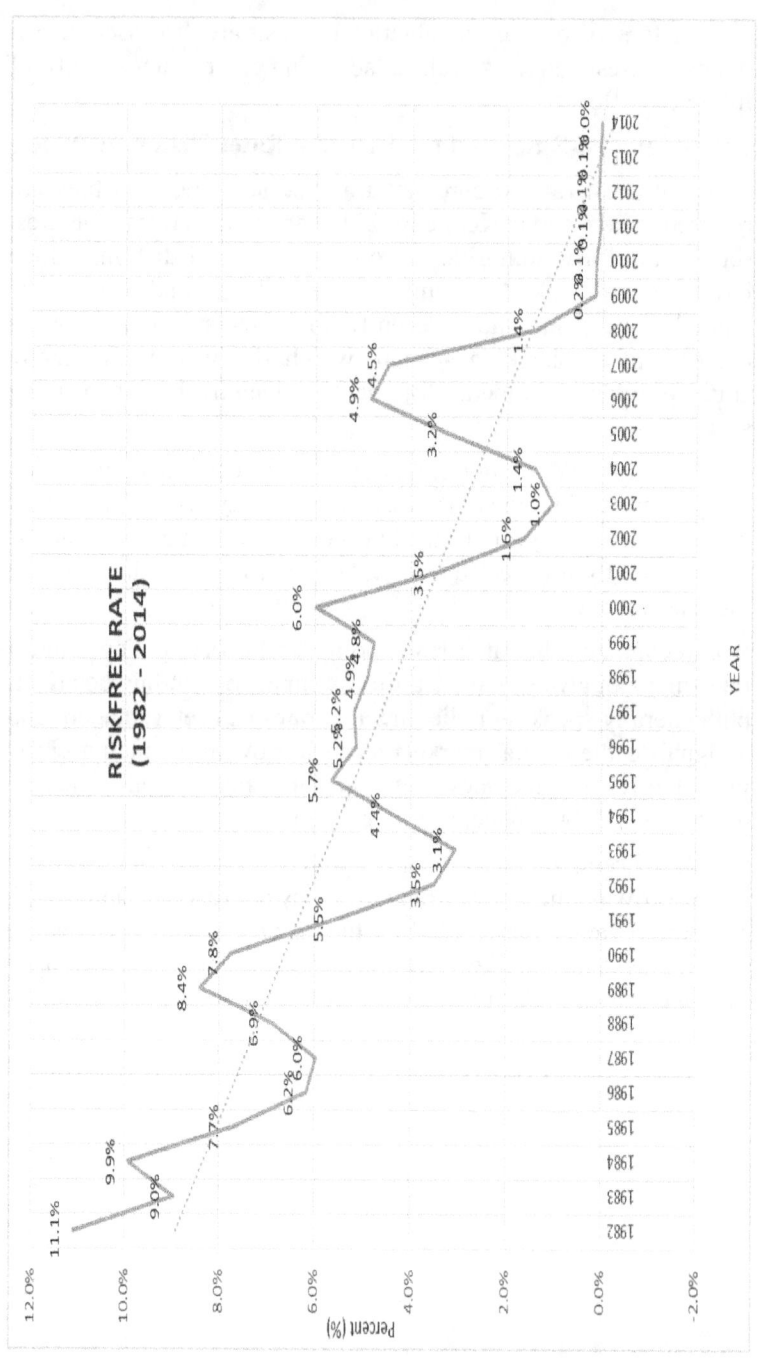

Data Source: Federal Reserve Releases (2015)

The straight line running through the chart is simply a linear trend line.

Bond Values. It is apparent from the chart that over the past 30+ years policy interest rates as exhibited by this *riskfree* rate have trended downwards. This is important because much of the valuation literature reviewed above relies upon a measure of the *riskfree* rate, but which can lead to distortions in terms of overvaluation when yields decline. As bond prices are inversely related to yields, the secular decline in the *riskfree* rate suggests a concomitant *rise* in bond values that may be disconnected from underlying fundamentals. Overvaluation or a "bond bubble" is of particular concern given the emergence of *negative interest rates* in debt markets worldwide as of 2016.

The formula for the present value (PV) of a bond can be consulted in a finance textbook or a spreadsheet program, but the key inputs are r_m the *market* rate of interest*, r_c *the coupon rate of interest*, F the *face value* of the bond, M the *redemption value* of the bond at maturity, and n is the number of years. If the *market rate* is below the *coupon rate*, then the *present value* (or market value) of the bond is higher than the *face value* of the bond. (Shim, et al. 127)

*Note: The preferred term for "market" interest rate is "policy" interest rate because of the potentially strong influence monetary policy can have on yields.

Example. Starting with a base case: A 20-year bond with a coupon rate of 10% compounded semi-annually, a market rate of 10%, a face value of $100 and redemption value of $100. The present value of the bond is the face value=$100. Now assuming declining policy (market) interest rates over time. The coupon rate is unchanged at 10%, but the market rate has now declined to 3%. The bond value doubles, to approximately $205. If this decline in market rates occurs over a 10-year period, the bond value "grows" by virtue of the interest rate decline by over 7% per year, nominally (compound annual growth rate). A concern is that a policy interest rate-induced rise in the value of bonds over time does not properly reflect fundamental value, and suggesting a secular distortion of bond prices from the historical *riskfree* rate chart above.

Policy Interest Rate-Dependent Estimation of Financing Costs. As detailed above on financing costs, the discount rate/rate of return computed through a process of *estimation*. Much of the valuation literature reviewed above relies upon a measure of *policy interest rates* including the *riskfree rate* which are generally key data inputs in the estimation of these rates of return/discount rates. A problem with the use of the *riskfree rate* and policy-based interest rates is the possibility for misleading measures of rates of return and overvaluation as policy interest rates decline. The consequences of reliance on policy interest rates may be seen in a tendency towards secular excessive valuations in various markets not only in bonds but also in stocks. Possible overvaluation in stocks will be covered in the section on valuation of equities and the price-earnings ratio.

Adjusting for Uncertainty of Future Cash Flows

Expected Return [E(NPV)]. The calculation of NPV should ideally also incorporate *uncertainty* because the future cash flows of a particular investment are not known. When adjusting the net present value (NPV) from above for uncertainty as measured by *probable* future cash flows, the NPV becomes the *expected value* of NPV, or E (NPV). The E(NPV) may be referred to as an "expected return" although E(NPV) is not a *rate* of return. Also, the E(NPV) should not be confused with the *expected rate of return* to be discussed in the section below. A general formula for E(NPV) with net cash flows in perpetuity can be written as:

$$E(NPV) = \sum_{t=1}^{t=\infty} E(NCFt)/(1+r)^t - IC$$

...where $E(NCF_t)$ is the *expected net cash flow* in each year of the project, r is the *"required" rate of return/discount rate* as decided upon by investors, and *IC* is the initial cost outlay. *(Note: the term *required rate of return* is discussed further below).

Example. It might be easier to visualize the process of arriving at E(NPV) from expected net cash flow E(NCF) by referring to the table below which shows *probable future net cash flows* and the associated probabilities for years 1, 2 and 3 of a hypothetical 3-year project.

3-Year Project: Probable Future Net Cash Flows

Year	Probabilities			E(NCFt)	E(PVt)
	0.3	0.4	0.3		
1	10	20	30	20	18.2
2	15	25	35	25	20.7
3	18	28	40	28.6	21.5
∑E(PVt)					60.3
Initial Cost Outlay					-50.0
E(NPV)					10.3

Assume that the required rate of return/discount rate for this project is **10%** and its proposed initial cost is **-50** (this cost figure should be shown as a negative).

The logic is explained for **year 1**: There is a 30% probability of the project's probable future net cash flow of being as low as 10 or as high as 30; in year 1 there is also a 40% probability of the project's probable future net cash flow of being 20. (Note that the sum of the probabilities in each year should be 1 or 100%).

E(NCF$_t$). The figures shown in the E(NCF) column are computed by multiplying* the *probabilities* by the *net cash flows* in each year then summing them. So, for **year 1**, the expected net cash flow is 20 (=.30x10 + .4x20 + .3x30). For year 2 and 3 the figures are 25 and 28.6, respectively.

*Note that in the context of the example provided in the next section below that *probability* x *net cash flow* defined as a *"payoff"* can also be referred to as an *expected payoff*.

E(PV$_t$). The *expected present value* is now computed as follows: First, the E(NCF) for each year (20, 25, and 28.6 from the E(NCF) column) is discounted by the required rate of return r (which we have assumed is 10%). For year 1, this is $[20/(1+.10)^1]$, year 2 this is $[25/(1+.10)^2]$, and year 3 this is $[28.6/(1+.10)^3]$. The column E(PV$_t$) shows the results, 18.2, 20.7 and 21.5 for years 1, 2 and 3, respectively. Summing these three figures, 18.2 + 20.7 + 21.5 gives us $\sum$E(PV$_t$) which is a sum total of about 60 for all three years discounted to the present (differences due to rounding).

E(NPV). Finally, we deduct the initial cost (cash outlay) of 50 to arrive at the *expected net present value* of 10.3.

Expected Rate of Return and Probability

When uncertainty is factored into the computation of rates of return, the rate of return is preceded by the term "expected." To begin, the concept of "expected payoff" is explained.

Expected Payoff Concept. When one is told that a particular *speculative* investment has a 99% chance (i.e. probability) of loss, the investment would likely be viewed unfavorably. However, a key point that can be overlooked is that the *probability* of the occurrence of an event is not enough information to determine the *expected return* of the investment. The concept of "expected payoff" is necessary to complete an analysis of "riskiness." *Expected payoff* is the *probability* multiplied by the *payoff*; in a financial context, the *payoff* is the projected individual *net cash flow* (whether positive, or negative in the case of a projected loss) that is attached to a particular probability.

Expected Rate of Return: Example with Expected ROI. To illustrate the above, we revisit the concept of *rate of return on investment* (often abbreviated as *return on investment* or ROI) which was covered in the section on *prior period costs*. These ROI computations can be transformed into future costs involving decision-making about a contemplated asset purchase; in this case the ROI could be referred to as "expected rate of return on investment," or E(ROI).

To take an extreme example, suppose that a call option on a stock has a 99% probability of *total loss* ("total loss" meaning that the initial amount paid will be entirely lost). A speculator has $100 and is considering purchasing the option. Is this speculative investment worth making? If there is a high enough *payoff* associated with the remaining 1% probability, *in theory* the investment might still be worth making. Supposing that there is a 99% chance of losing the original $100 paid to purchase the option, but that there is a 1% chance of a positive $30,000 payoff (i.e. positive net cash inflow): Then the *expected payoff* is $201 [=(.99x-100)+(.01x30000)], the *expected profit* is $101 (=201-100), and the *expected rate of return* on that investment is 101% (=201/101), or about a doubling.

*Notes:

-The probability of the individual payoffs should total to 1.

-The term "speculative" is distinguished from "investment" due to the assessed level of risk; opinions may differ on what should be called "speculative" and what should be called an "investment."

To balance out the previous argument, consider another option presented to the speculator with $100: A 60% chance of *doubling* one's money (from $100 to $200), and a 40% chance of a total loss (-$100). Initially the investment may seem favorable, but the *expected rate of return* E(ROI) of *negative* 20% indicates poor prospects.

Risk and Uncertainty: Some History and Commentary

The remarkable topic of risk and uncertainty requires a full book of its own, but a few highlights are noted here.

Measures of Riskiness of Assets

Volatility as a Measure of Risk. Revisiting the above discussion regarding the seminal work of Markowitz (1952) and others (re: Capital Asset Pricing Model CAPM and modifications), the term "risk" tends to be associated with a stock *volatility* definition in which a stock is riskier the greater its movement relative to the overall market (as reflected in the "beta" β). In a "down" market a $\beta>1$ suggests losses greater than for a broadly diversified portfolio representative of the market.

Probability of Firm Cash Flows. A *volatility-as-risk* definition may have limitations. If the investor's objective is to understand the risks associated with the underlying business fundamentals, including the prospects for rising dividend income and debt service capacity, risk might be better measured by analysis of a company's financial performance and *equity income generating capacity* (Kennedy 2014, 2015). Dorsey (2004) states: "We think it's better to assess risk by looking at the company, rather than by looking at the stock, and that a firm's riskiness is determined by the likelihood that it will or won't generate the cash flows that we're forecasting."(145)

Economic Theory. Moreover, a thorough understanding of underlying economic fundamentals, including monetary factors and monetary theory may provide additional clues as to the true magnitude of risks involved in investing. The study of economic cycles and "booms" and "busts" (recessions and expansions/recoveries) is also considered worthwhile towards a better understanding of the probabilities of future events. It should be noted that as of the early 20th century some theories of cycles are not considered mainstream although there may be value in incorporating concepts of various theories into economic analysis nevertheless; one such example is Austrian business cycle theory (Mises 1912, Huerta de Soto 2012).

Probability Theory. It should be emphasized that much of the literature on risk assumes fundamentally that economic and financial phenomena more or less conform to a *normal probability distribution*. However, the validity of this assumption may be questionable and risks may be much larger than the normal probability distribution might suggest. This point is addressed also in the Appendix.

Historical Note: Risk and Profit/Returns. Adam Smith (1776) pointed out the relationship between uncertainty and the rate of profit: "In all the different employments of stock, the ordinary rate of profit varies more or less with the certainty or uncertainty of the returns"….and the "ordinary rate of profit always rises more or less with the risk."…"to compensate it (the risk) completely, the common returns ought, over and above the ordinary profits of stock, not only to make up for all occasional losses, but to afford a surplus profit to the adventurers (i.e. in the hazardous trades like smugglers where the bankruptcies are most frequent) of the same nature with the profit of insurers. But if the common returns were sufficient for all this, bankruptcies would not be more frequent in these than in other trades." (99)

The pioneering work of Frank Knight (1921), introduced a definition of profit that integrates uncertainty: "…the difference between an *expected return* and a *realized return*, as intimately connected with uncertainty, but as a consequence of uncertainty, not as a reward for submitting to uncertainty."(Friedman 1986: 281) (Italics added).

Irving Fisher (1930) also clearly incorporated the concept of risk into his definition of *profits* which is noted in the historical essay in the Appendix.

The topic of risk and uncertainty is highly relevant to the next measure of rate of return, capitalization rates, as detailed in the next section.

Rates of Return in Capitalization Theory

Capitalization theory also involves valuation but has a somewhat different history which incorporates the concept of risk and uncertainty as detailed in the previous section.

Rate of Return Measure #3: Capitalization Rates.

Risk and Required Return Concept. Capitalization rates are a simple practical tool for the valuation of closely-held companies (Tuller 1994). The *capitalization rate* ("cap" rate for short) is a form of *required rate of return* employed to arrive at an estimated value for the firm that historically has reflected an adjustment for the assessed *risk* of the particular enterprise; the risk being associated with the probability of failure of the business (meaning future cash flows/income would cease).

A body of literature developed beginning in the early 20th century to define various appropriate risk categories that could be used as a guideline as a minimum *required rate of return* when factoring in risk (Badger 1926, Dewing 1953, Schilt 1982, Pratt 1989). The "low risk" category might describe an established and long-standing stable business with seasoned management (capitalization rate of 10-12%), while the highest risk level might describe a start-up single owner microbusiness in a highly-competitive industry with unproven management (capitalization rate of 50% to 100%).

Valuation of Perpetuity Approach. As part of the process of valuation of a business, in addition to identifying an appropriate capitalization rate/required rate of return incorporating risk, a common and simple approach is to assume that the income of the business will continue in perpetuity. The *valuation of a perpetuity* (V_p) formula is:

$$V_p = \pi/r$$

Where π is a single year's *net income* of the firm, and r is the *capitalization rate* (as well as the *required rate of return* that the buyer/investor in the business expects). For example, for a business in a very low-risk category, the capitalization rate might be assumed at 10%. With a projected annual net income of 100, the firm's value would be estimated at (100/0.10)=1000, or "ten times net income." For a firm with the same projected annual income but in the higher risk category with an assumed capitalization rate of 50%, the value would decline accordingly due to the risk of failure: 100/.50=200, or "two times net income."

Historically, the capitalization rate was not necessarily related to the *discounting* of future net income to present value. Later, the estimation of capitalization rates aligned with that of the *discount rate* in corporate finance, where a *risk premium* is added to the rate of an assumed *risk-free* investment such as U.S. Treasuries of a comparable maturity (Schilt 1982, Pratt 1989). See the discussion elsewhere on the *riskfree* interest rate.

Weighting. In addition to adding a risk factor, the *weighted* capitalization rate can take into account the proportion of debt and equity in the purchase price of the asset and their respective costs (Coltman 1989:62). For example, if the purchase price of a business was financed with half equity and half debt, with the cost of the debt of 20% (10% interest and a factor to cover the return of the principal balance of the loan of 10% or 1/10 each year for a 10-year loan, for example), and a required return on equity of 25% (which includes the risk factor of say 5%), the weighted capitalization rate would be computed at 22.5% (=50% debt x 10% + 50% equity x 35%).

Application of Capitalization Rates to Income Real Estate

In commercial real estate valuation of the early 21st century, capitalization rates (abbreviated the "cap rate") may be employed in the *income capitalization approach*. The income approach capitalizes *net operating income* (NOI) to arrive at an indication of value. Note however that there is not necessarily an adjustment for *risk* as described above in the chronology of capitalization theory.

The *direct capitalization* approach divides the NOI by an appropriate cap rate according to the *valuation of a perpetuity* (V_p) formula stated earlier, $V_p = \pi/r$; in this case π is the *net operating income* (NOI) of the building for a 12-month period, and a final estimate of the appropriate capitalization rate is determined by a *sales comparison* and other approaches. Sales of comparable

69

buildings (recent sale dates and similar locations as well as building sizes and stabilized occupancy) are examined, and interviews may be conducted with real estate brokers in the area.

Example: Valuation by Direct Capitalization of NOI. An example is provided here to illustrate the direct capitalization approach. The forecasted income of a commercial real estate building at the turn of the 21th century (amounts in U.S. currency, Western United States circa 2000-2001) is presented here (the table is referred to as an Annual Income Forecast)

TABLE: ANNUAL INCOME FORECAST

GROSS RENTAL INCOME	300000		
Vacancy (5% of Gross)	15000		
Effective Gross Income (EGI)	285000		
EXPENSE DETAIL	TOTAL	% of EGI	Landlord
Fixed Expense			*Note
Taxes	21375	0.075	
Insurance	7125	0.025	
Operating Expenses			
Common Area Mgt (CAM)	14250	0.05	
Utilities	1425	0.1	0.05
Ground Maintenance	1425	0.005	
Maintenance/Repairs	428	0.03	0.05
Misc Other	143	0.01	0.05
Reserve Expenses	8550	0.03	
(flooring, painting, roofing, elevator, heating/cooling)			
TOTAL EXPENSES	54720	0.325	
NET OPERATING INCOME (NOI)	230280		

*Notes: Landlord share, only if less than 100%, is noted. The gross rental income= net rentable area (square feet) x rental rate per square foot per month x 12 months.

As seen from the Annual Income Forecast table above, the property's NOI is $230,280 for the 12-month period.

Derivation of the Capitalization Rate. The capitalization rate is obtained by analysis of comparable sales of properties (sales prices and NOI based on rentable area and rental rates, etc.). The *perpetuity valuation* formula from above $V_p = \pi/r$ can be rearranged, with the recent sales prices (P) replacing the valuation (V_p) as follows:

$$r = \pi/P$$

The capitalization rate can be estimated from an analysis of comparable sales in the real estate market. The *indicated market value* of the property is obtained by dividing the NOI of the building by the final estimate of capitalization rate which is estimated to be 9.25% at the time:

$$\$230,280 / .0925 = \$2,489,514$$

Note. Alternative measures of value can also be obtained simply by the comparable sales analysis (called the *sales approach*) without the need for a capitalization rate. The *cost approach* is another method of estimating the value by estimation of the cost to build a similar property.

Comparison of Rates of Return. The rates of return at the time (circa 2000-2001) are compared:
(1) Internal rate of return (IRR)
(2) Financing costs (aka cost of capital/borrowing rate for debt);
(3) Capitalization rate.

Internal Rate of Return: 8.4%. This IRR was computed based on the above valuation (which is also assumed to be the purchase price) of $2.49 million and a stabilized NOI for 30 years of $230,280.

Capitalization Rate Estimate: 9.25% (from above)

Financing Costs/Cost of Capital (Debt). The table below presents financing costs (aka cost of capital) for various types of debt financing during the time period (figures are approximate):

SUMMARY OF FINANCING COSTS	Annual Rate
10-Yr Treasury Bond	5.30%
30-Year Treasury Bond	5.70%
Corporate Bond (Aaa - Baa)	7%-8%
Bank Borrowing Rate*	7%-8%

*Note: Bank borrowing rate is the annual interest rate of a bank commercial mortgage [75%-80% loan-to-value (LTV) on a first mortgage, 5 year call and 25 year amortization with a debt service coverage ratio of 1.25 are assumed].

Policy Interest Rates and Returns-to-Valuation Analysis (RVA): Real Estate

The following analysis employing a simple example in commercial real estate markets illustrates a possible systemic problem with the lowering of policy interest rates leading to overvaluation of assets. "Overvaluation" is defined as growth in asset values that is not aligned with the growth in rates of return on cost, referred to as a *rate of return-to-valuation gap* (abbreviated as *returns-to-valuation* gap, or RVG). This key concept will be discussed at length further below and in Part II of the book.

Note that '000s will be abbreviated as "K" (i.e. 230,000 becomes 230K). Key changes in the figures within the Lending Dynamics table below are surrounded by a bold border.

LENDING DYNAMICS Measures and Rates	Starting Point	Stage 1: Drop in Interest Rates	Stage 2: Increased MV
Valuation / Market Prices	2,489,514	2,489,514	3,111,892
Annual NOI - unchanged	230,280	230,280	230,280
Capitalization Rate	0.0925	0.0925	0.074
Bank Loan Rate	0.075	0.055	0.055
Loan Amount (25-yr amortization)	2,000,000	2,500,000	2,500,000
Debt Service (approx. annual)	150,000	137,500	137,500
Debt Service Coverage Ratio	1.54	1.67	1.67
Loan-to-Value (LTV)	0.80	1.00	0.80

Starting Point (Column 1 of figures). The first column of figures is the "starting point" which was explained above. The property is valued at $2.49 million, the annual NOI is $230K, the capitalization rate based on market analysis was found to be 9.25%. At the time, bank loan rates were in the 7-8% range as seen in the cost of financing table above. At a 7.5% bank loan rate (borrowing rate), the borrower could afford to service debt on a $2 million commercial mortgage because the debt service (approximate annual amount of debt service at a 25-year amortization) is $150K which produces a debt service coverage ratio (DSC) ratio of a reasonable 1.54 (=230K/150K). At this starting point the loan-to-value (LTV) is a still-acceptable 80% (=2 million/2.49 million).

Stage 1: Lowered Policy Interest Rates and LTV. The second column of figures is "Stage 1" when policymakers decide to lower interest rates to stimulate economic growth. The mechanism is not described here but monetary policy tools are capable of inducing a general lowering of bank loan rates, as well as other interest rates (referred to herein as "policy interest rates."). In this example, the bank loan rates have declined by two percentage points, at 5.5%. This lower interest rate helps lower the debt service on a *larger* loan amount of $2.5 million. In fact, note that although the loan amount increased by $500K, the debt service has *declined* to $137.5K due to the lower borrowing rate. The debt service coverage ratio has also improved to 1.67 from the previous 1.54. However, there is one "snag" in this situation: The value of the property has not risen. Therefore, the loan-to-value (LTV) is *too high* at 1.00 (100% of the value of the property).

This improved affordability in debt service due to the lower interest rates may subsequently begin to influence the overall marketplace and over time, other properties are purchased with financing at the lower bank loan rate. It may not unusual for this situation to result in an eventual rise in market values for comparable properties over time, as well as additional construction activity which is often the objective of policymakers.

The question might arise how any borrowers could have received financing if the loan-to-value ratios were too high initially. Some borrowers might push sales prices higher by bringing in more *equity* capital into the financing mix so as to meet LTV guidelines; due to the debt affordability higher prices for properties may remain attractive for potential buyers with extra equity capital to invest. Some banks may also stretch guidelines somewhat due to pressure to meet loan goals. Also important to consider is the logic of the capitalization approach: If soft market conditions from oversupply of commercial space cause NOIs to stagnate or even fall, as long as sales prices are rising, *lower* capitalization rates may be derived due to application of the $r=\pi/P$ approach. As capitalization rates decline, a widening gap between rates of return and valuations can accelerate.

Stage 2: Market Values Rising. As a result of the affordability and chain of events in stage 1 and described above, assume that general market activity has resulted in a 25% increase in property values although there has been *no change* in the annual NOI (reflecting for example no change in demand for commercial space relative to the supply of space opening up due to new construction of commercial real estate spurred on by the lower interest rates).

At this point, a new appraisal of the property is ordered and based on this 25% increase in overall market values (per square foot basis), and the unchanged NOI, the appraiser evaluates the capitalization rate. Recall from above the derivation of the capitalization rate by analysis of comparable sales of properties as follows: $r=\pi/P$ where P is based on overall sales prices for comparable properties in the market and π is the estimated NOI of those properties.

In a market in which rental rates for comparable properties have risen overall by 25%, and assuming that the NOI of properties have remained *unchanged*, application of the formula results in a decline in the capitalization rate. In Stage 2 (column 3) the capitalization rate is adjusted *downwards* to 7.4%.

When a capitalization rate of 7.4% is applied to the unchanged NOI of the property, the property value is revalued upwards to $3.1 million. Recall in Stage 1 that the loan-to-value ratio was too high for the loan to qualify for financing. Now, as can be seen at the bottom of column 3, the LTV now nicely fits within bank guidelines for financing.

A tentative conclusion could be suggested at this juncture: Through a process of declining interest rates, real estate asset values may be inflated. Banks may find themselves lending more capital to finance the asset than the rates of return generated by the asset would justify. Subsequently, borrowers may experience financial hardships and banks may suffer loan losses if the additional construction and lending activity stimulated by the lower interest rates results in an oversupply of properties with excessive vacancies. On a possible systemic problem of overlending due to the dynamics as described above, the following point by Sigurjónsson (2015) might be relevant: "For more than half a century, Iceland has suffered from serious monetary problems including inflation, hyperinflation, devaluations, an asset bubble and ultimately the collapse of its banking sector in 2008. Other countries have faced similar problems. Since 1970, bank crisis have occurred 147 times in 114 countries causing serious reductions in output and increases in debt. "(2015:9)

Rates of Return and Valuation of Equities

Three examples of rates of return are presented here in the context of valuation methods for equities.

The rate of return applicable in the first two examples of valuation of equities is the *required rate of return*, or the rate of return that investors expect to receive for their investments.

The second rate of return measure applicable incorporates risk in a manner resembling the logic of capitalization theory as detailed in the section on risk and uncertainty above. The third rate of return measure is a ratio of income (EPS) to price (of the stock); this approach resembles the *valuation of a perpetuity* method as described in the section on valuation in income real estate above, where a measure of income (the NOI) was compared to the price of the asset (the real estate).

Required Rate of Return

Valuation: Dividend in Perpetuity Approach. The valuation formula $V_p = \pi/r$ shown above can also be applied to valuing an individual stock according to its annual *dividend payment* in perpetuity and a *required rate of return*. The *net income* in this case is the *dividend*, and the rate of return is the *required (rate of) return* as specified by the investor. (Peters 2008: 33) For example, if the dividend payment is $1.00 per year, and the investor's required return were 10% (or 0.10), the value of the stock would in theory be worth $10 ($10=$1/.10).

Valuation: Rising Dividends in Perpetuity Approach. The above example assumes no change in dividend payments over time. However, since investors may desire *rising* growth of dividends over time, the well-known *Gordon Growth Model* (Gordon, 1962) is one version of a *dividend discount model* that provides a simple way to incorporate rising dividend growth into valuation of a perpetuity. This rising income stream is assumed to be at a *stable* growth rate; note that the model is most applicable to established firms with a consistent record of dividend payments:

$$PV_p = d\,(1+g)/(r\text{-}g)$$

Where PV_p is the present perpetuity value of the stock, d is the current dividend per share, r is the *required rate of return* for equity investors, and g is the growth rate of dividends in perpetuity. The model's limitations are noted by Damodaran (194).

Rates of Return Factoring in Risk

Valuation: An n-Year Discount Model and Free Cash Flow. A practitioner variation of stock valuation uses *free cash flow* of the firm instead of dividends and an *n-year free cash flow discount model*. Free cash flow (also referred to as net cash flow or NCF) is typically defined as:

Cash Flow from Operations less Capital Expenditures

In the *n-year free cash flow discount model*, the perpetuity value is only calculated *after* a specified time period in the future, for example after 10-years: The *perpetuity value* from year 11 forward is discounted to the present using the formula above (PV1). The discounted present value of the individual cash flows for the first 10 years of the model (years 1 through 10) is calculated separately using the standard formula for discounting to present value (PV2). Then, the two present value figures (PV1-*perpetuity* and PV2-*n periods*) are added together to arrive at the firm's total equity value. To convert to per share value, the total equity value is then divided by the number of shares outstanding of the firm (Dorsey: 145).

Relative Firm Risk Measures. The rate of return/discount rate employed in the above approach to valuation is based on the level of risk of the firm relative to a measure of average risk. As of the turn of the 21st century, the range from lowest to highest risk firms was between 9% to 15%, with 10.5% being the discount rate for an average company (Dorsey: 146-7)

Rates of Return as Net Income (Earnings) to Price

The discussion below begins with a brief introduction of valuation of equities as measured by the Price-Earnings ratio. Note that *net income* is synonymous to *earnings* in the context of equities.

Valuation of Equities: Price-Earnings Ratio. The price-earnings ratio (PE Ratio or PER) is a common measure of valuation of equities in which the stock price of a firm is divided by earnings per share (EPS) of a firm. There are numerous variations of the PE Ratio which can be referenced in the finance and valuation literature. Notably, the Price-Cash Flow ratio replaces earnings with a measure of the firm's cash flow.

A notable variant of the PE ratio is the Cyclically-Adjusted Price Earnings Ratio (PE10 or CAPE) for the S&P 500 stock index from 1983.1 to 2015.10 (chart may be truncated due to space considerations). The CAPE is an indicator of the PE ratio developed by Shiller (2015).

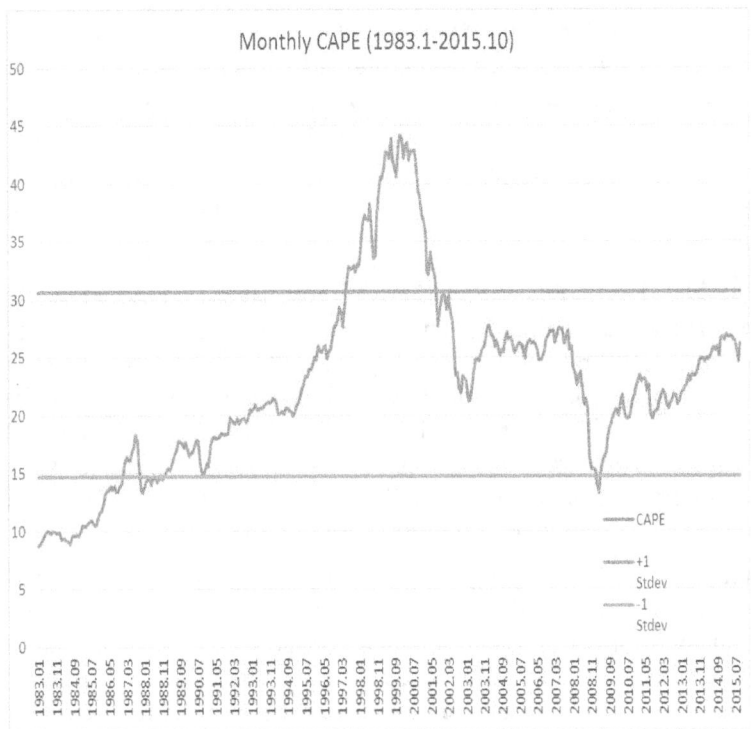

Monthly CAPE (1983.1-2015.10)

Source: Shiller (2015)

The mean (average) for the period was 22.7, with a standard deviation of approximately 8. The high of the monthly data (not shown) was 44 in December of 1999, and a low of 8.76 in the first month of the sample, January 1983. The chart shows a "band" of 1 standard deviation around the mean as a reference as a rough indicator of the central tendency of the data (assuming normality).

Earnings-Price Ratio (EPR). In order to arrive at a measure of rate of return, we look at the inverse of the PE ratio which can be called the Earnings-Price ratio (EPR); the EPR can be viewed as a kind of per-share *rate of return* measure for equities.

Recall the perpetuity valuation formula from the section above on capitalization theory. This relationship can also be applied to the valuation of equities. The variables of the formula $V_p = \pi/r$ can be rearranged as before, then renamed so that the stock price (P) replaces the valuation (V_p), and π (which was NOI for real estate) is replaced by a measure of net income for stocks called *earnings per share*. A capitalization rate *r* for equities can then be computed and is called the earnings-price ratio or EPR as follows: $EPR = \pi/P$.

The EPR is shown as percentages in the next section below together with the PER. The EPR high was at the beginning of the observation period (January 1983), and the lows were reached primarily during the period 2000-2001. The mean for the entire period was 5%, with a standard deviation of 2%.

Returns-to-Valuation Analysis for Equities.

PE Ratio and EPR. The chart below juxtaposes both the price-earnings (PE) ratio as measured by the CAPE and EPR from above. Note that by looking at the CAPE alone it appears that the lofty valuations of the turn of the 21st century have subsided and valuations have returned to a more "normal" level if defined as the long-term mean (of about 22.7) or within a standard deviation band as shown above of roughly between 30 and 15.

However, when viewing both variables together, a secular trend of divergence is apparent. The two variables are inversely related and therefore mirror one another inversely (one variable rising when the other falls); however, a neutral valuation scenario would imply that stock price valuations and their rates of return would be roughly aligned with one another horizontally (even when taking into account considerable variability). Thus, a divergence between the two suggests that while stocks are yielding less in terms of rates of return relative to their prices, they are being valued higher: That is, a possible systemic overvaluation scenario over the long term.

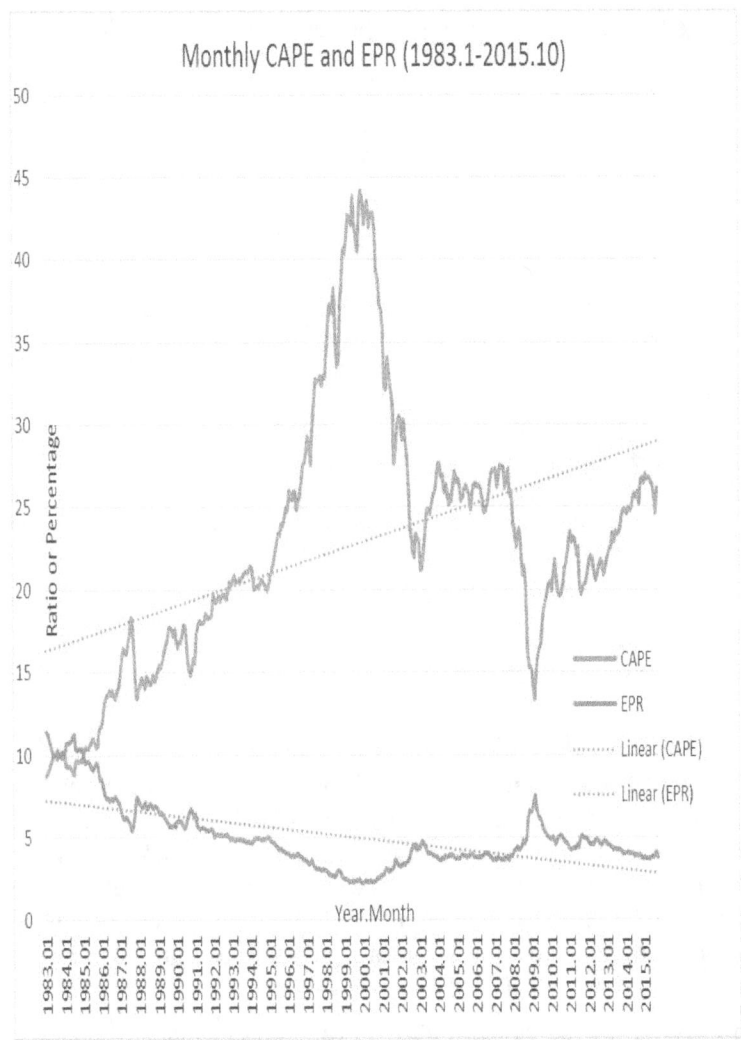

Source: Shiller (2015)

For purposes of illustration but employing actual data from the same series, now compare the above chart with a similar chart of the CAPE and EPR but for a small subsample (1994.3 to 1995.1) where the individual variables hovered roughly along their own horizontal trend lines, thereby roughly aligning with one another;. There were a number of similar sub-periods but this one was selected because during that time period the CAPE was the closest to the long-term mean of 22.

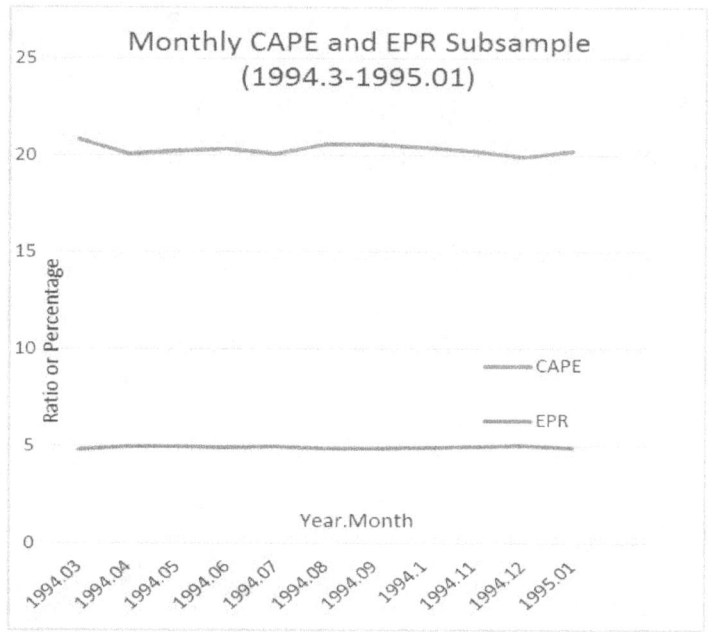

Source: Shiller (2015)

Note on EPR Measures. Stock buybacks, a feature of 21st century corporate landscape, can result in increased earnings on a per share basis, giving the impression that higher stock prices are justified. As policy interest rates decline, firms can benefit by the lower borrowing costs which allow them to borrower cheaply to buy back their shares, further inflating their apparent rate of return as measured by the EPR.

In closing, just as detailed above in the commentary on income real estate and bank lending on real estate, the problem of overvaluation in equities also is assumed to occur from a "disconnect" or "gap" between the valuation of assets and the underlying rates of return generated by those same assets. Such an overvaluation error can lead to asset bubbles and subsequent crashes in capital markets as well. For example, *equity markets* can be impacted by the mismatch between the income-generating capacity of the financial entities (businesses) and their valuations as reflected in their stock prices. Another approach to the *returns-*

to-valuation analysis (RVA) for equities is detailed in the upcoming Part II of this book.

PART II.
RATES OF RETURN FOR FINANCIAL ENTITIES

Rate of Return on Cost (RRC). Part I provides an overview of concepts of rates of return, drawing from historical examples. This section constructs a specific rate of return measure called the *rate of return on cost* or RRC, applicable to financial entities as defined in Part I, first for Category #1A organizations (e.g. firms/businesses), and later for Category #1B individuals.

This returns measure is considered to be *financial*, although an economic dimension can be added (see Appendix 1).

The term *rate of return on cost* should also be distinguished from Irving Fisher's *rate of return over cost*, already noted above in the historical overview; Fisher's rate of return is an equalizing rate of return when comparing the present value (present worth) of two income streams (Fisher 1930).

CONSTRUCTING THE RRC

Rate of Return (RRC). The rate of return on cost (RRC) is defined as *Net Cash Flow net of acquisitions* (or "net net cash flow", NNCF) divided by the total cost of production (as a cash outflow) in the *same* fiscal year. The definitions of each variable are detailed below.

$$RRC = NNCF / Cost$$

Both figures are flows occurring in the same fiscal year. For example, in a given fiscal year if revenues are 100, and total cost is 90, then the NNCF is 10 (=100-90). The RRC would then therefore be 10/90 or 11%. The total cost is the sum of the Cost of Production items in the Net Benefit Accounting Framework table below. The rate of return on cost is expected to vary from year to year with a high level of unpredictability and variability.

Causality. Although easily overlooked, there is an assumed causality between the variables NNCF and the Cost. The relationship between these two variables suggests purposeful action by financial entities in that that costs are incurred in order to generate the returns, and that this is an ongoing process.

Return (Net Benefit). The numerator, NNCF, is a measure of *net benefit* of the rates of return relationship as presented in the Definitions of Part I. NNCF is also the cash flow *return* (not the *rate* of return) arising from the cost of production outflows in the same period (fiscal year). Both NNCF and Cost are *flows*, and cash flow is used to represent physical quantities (cash), rather than *accrual* figures which have an important basis is Generally Accepted Accounting Principles (GAAP).

Note that the term "profit" is often considered to be the numerator for the return on a particular investment. The problem with profit is in its accrual definition, all of the resource outflows that are necessary for the business/economic activity are not included. NNCF is considered here to be a more comprehensive measure that accounts for the costs of production, measured in cash. If the term "profit" were to be used in place of NNCF, then "cash flow profit" might be an approximation, although the framework as presented herein may not be as clear.

The following table titled "Net Benefit Accounting Framework" clarifies the understanding of the relationship of the variables. This accounting framework incorporates the framework from Kennedy (2014) and (2015) to account for *equity income* (see below for detail), as well as the *source of repayment* for debt service (principal + interest). The figures are hypothetical and are for a single fiscal year (or calendar year when the fiscal year and the calendar year are the same).

NET BENEFIT ACCOUNTING FRAMEWORK

Revenues	100
LESS: Cost of Production (Cash Outflow):	
Cost of Goods Sold (COGS)	70
Selling, General & Administrative (S,G&A)	10
Capital Expenditures (Capex)	6
Acquisitions,other	4
Subtotal-Cost of Production	90
=Net Net Cash Flow (NNCF)*	10
Less: Dividends/Distributions	2
NNCF -D (Source of Repayment for Debt Service)	8
Less: Principal Repayment (P)	2
Less: Interest Payment (i)	1
NNCF after Debt Service	5

*NNCF is also referred to as *equity income* and is also the *net benefit* or *return* of the firm.

Note that depreciation is non-cash and is not included as a cash outflow in this framework. Also it should be emphasized that *non-recurring items* of cash income such as special subsidies and bailouts are not included. *Non-cash items* are detailed in Kennedy (2014:13, and Note 9:16).

Equity Income (NNCF) as the Return. *Equity income* is Net Net Cash Flow (NNCF) in the line above dividends/distributions, and is the "net benefit" or return (not the *rate* of return which is a ratio). Equity income is a net cash inflow to the firm after its costs are deducted from its revenues, and is viewed as attributable to the firm's owners /equity holders; equity income remains a *potential* source of payment for dividends/distributions to the owners/equity investors regardless of whether dividends/distributions are actually paid out. The line item "dividends/distributions" below equity income is what is physically paid to the equity investor(s)/business owners for their investment, a physical "return" on their investment. For additional detail on equity income, see Kennedy (2014).

Debt Service SOR: NNCF – D is the primary source of repayment (SOR) for debt service (principal P + interest i) of the debt holders/lenders/bondholders (Kennedy 2015).

For comparison purposes, a simple accrual-basis income statement is provided here. Hypothetical net profit/earnings for a single fiscal year of 19 can be contrasted with the NNCF figure of 10 above.

Income Statement (Accrual Basis)	
Revenues	100
Less: Cost of Goods Sold/Cost of Sales	70
= Gross Profit	30
Less: Selling, General & Administrative (S,G&A)	10
Less: Interest/Finance Costs	1
Net Profit/Earnings (Accrual-based)	19

The income statement is accrual-basis and does not show certain items of cost to the firm such as capital expenditures and acquisitions that would appear on a balance sheet or cash flow statement.

VARIABLES: DETAIL

Revenues. For simplicity, *accrual* revenues are used in the computation, although it recognized that accrual revenues differ from cash revenues and that a significant portion of (accrual) revenues could be tied up in receivables and have not been received as cash -therefore the cash cost of production is considered to be an estimate. While adjustments could be made to account for this difference, it is believed that accrual revenues are a reasonable approximation of the (final) cash revenues, perhaps more so for established firms examined here. Note that the NNCF figure is net of any cash outflows due to increases of receivables, so the RRC does not exclude this source of cash outflow.

Moreover, estimating based on accrual revenues is reasonably conservative. In the example above, if due to uncollected (or uncollectable) receivables, for example, cash revenues are 900 instead of the 100 of accrual revenues, then the actual cash cost of production would have been 80 instead. While more accurate from a cash flow perspective, the RRC would be higher at 12.5% (10/80= 12.5%) than using accrual revenues.

Cost. As shown in the chart above, the principal items of cost are: Cost of Goods Sold/Cost of Sales, Selling, General & Administrative Costs, Capital Expenditures, and Acquisitions. The cost is a physical (cash) outflow of all resources that are involved in the productive activities of the firm. These resources are reported on the annual financial statements of the firm including the cash flow statement. Cash outflows for *capital expenditures* and *acquisitions* would be considered the investment portion of the cost in the traditional sense of investment in fixed capital; the technical and other skills that are used to purchase, operate, and maintain the equipment as well as the *support services* that insure that the fixed capital provide a revenue to the firm (e.g. selling, general and administrative costs) are intertwined with the fixed capital. In a sufficiently advanced technological state fixed capital might be self-built and self-maintained without human support; in such a case, the portion of costs owing to human input may decline. However the costs may be classified, these costs are assumed to be associated with the productive activities of the business towards generating a *net benefit* or *return* (i.e. the NNCF) each year of operation.

Deriving the Return: NNCF

NNCF is *net cash flow* (NCF) (or alternatively called *free cash flow* or *FCF*) after deducting the cost of acquisitions, intangibles and other key investments. NCF was covered in Kennedy (2014) as the best approximation of a cash flow measure, drawing from Hitchner (2011) and Rosenbaum and Pearl (2013). Hitchner (2011) uses the term *net cash flow* or *net free cash flow* (both abbreviated as NCF). The formula for NCF is Earnings before interest and taxes – taxes on EBIT at effective tax rate + depreciation – capital expenditures plus/minus changes in working capital. (2011:500).

Rosenbaum and Pearl (2013) compute free cash flow starting with earnings before interest and after taxes (EBIAT). Their formula for FCF is: FCF=EBIAT + Depreciation and Amortization -

Capex - increase/ (decrease) in net working capital (2013: 131, 163).

An alternative measure of NCF can be obtained by referring to a company's financial statements as follows:

NCO-Capex

NCO *is net cash from operations* from the *cash flow statement* of a company's financial statements, and capex is an abbreviation for *capital expenditures* (also from the cash flow statement, in the Investing section). NCO obtained from this source may roughly correspond to the formula above for NCF and FCF after adjusting for changes in net working capital but *before* deducting capex. Note that *depreciation* should not be used as a substitute for capital expenditures (Moody's 2000:4)

NCO can be titled in various ways, including "Net Cash provided from/Used in Operations" or similar language.

Acquisitions, Intangibles and Other Key Investments. NCF (FCF) is not typically reduced by investments other than capital expenditures. However, as presented in Kennedy (2014), a more comprehensive "net" figure for NCF would be to deducted acquisitions, intangibles and other key investments.

In addition to capital expenditures, there may be other types of investment expenditures necessary to achieve or maintain dominance in an industry. For example, if a firm tends to make recurring business acquisitions, it could be argued that in addition to capital expenditures, cash outflows for business acquisitions should also be deducted to arrive at a more accurate figure for NCF. Such acquisitions and investments can take many forms, and the terminology may also vary. This could include the following examples which in some cases may represent significant amounts:

Acquisition of licenses, technology and patents
Acquisition of interests/investments in JVs
Acquisition of investments in associates
Acquisition of investments in consolidated undertakings
Capitalization of software costs (not included in capex)
Investments in non-marketable equity investments
Purchases of certain intangible assets

Purchases of long-term investments

Additional Considerations

Short-term Liquid Investments and Securities. It should be emphasized that many firms will invest excess cash flow into short-term assets that could be described as moderately liquid, but that are not intended to add to productive activities of the business. Since these items appear as investments in the cash flow statement, investing section, they can be easily confused with capital expenditures, acquisitions or other key investments as detailed above. These types of liquid "investments" should not be included in the computation of NCF.

Accounting for Non-Cash Transactions. Non-cash income potentially overstates cash flow if not properly identified. And special care should be taken to improve the accuracy of cash flow measures. A few examples of non-cash items that can appear to inflate cash flow include: Income/undistributed earnings according to the *equity method* of accounting for investments, gains on inventory due to increased valuation, deferred and amortized gain on sale of assets in sale-leaseback accounting, unrealized gains on marketable equity securities, and minority interest income (Kennedy 2014).

RRC OF SELECTED NON-FINANCIAL FIRMS

Sample Selection. Publicly-traded non-financial firms were selected with geographic and sector diversification. Firms listed on either the NYSE or the NASDAQ have audited financial statements and filings with the U.S. Securities and Exchange Commission (SEC) which are expected to improve the quality of financial information. These filings are predominantly 20-F and 10-K reports.

Sectors and Sector Groupings. There are five sectors (*sector* is also often referred to as *industry*) with one or two subsectors represented within each sector:

Basic Materials Sector:
    (1) Oil & Gas Production

(2) Integrated Oil Companies
Consumer Goods Sector: Beverages-Production & Distribution:
Healthcare Sector: Pharmaceutical
Industrial Goods Sector: Diversified Machinery
Technology Sector:
(1) Semiconductors-Integrated circuits
(2) Communications equipment.

Sector Distribution
Geographic. The country refers generally to the legal jurisdiction of incorporation, as reported to the SEC. The firms selected were from Europe (France, Norway), North America (U.S.), South Africa, Asia (Chinese Taipei/Taiwan).
Market Capitalization. The total market capitalization of the firms is estimated at $US 635 billion as of 2015.

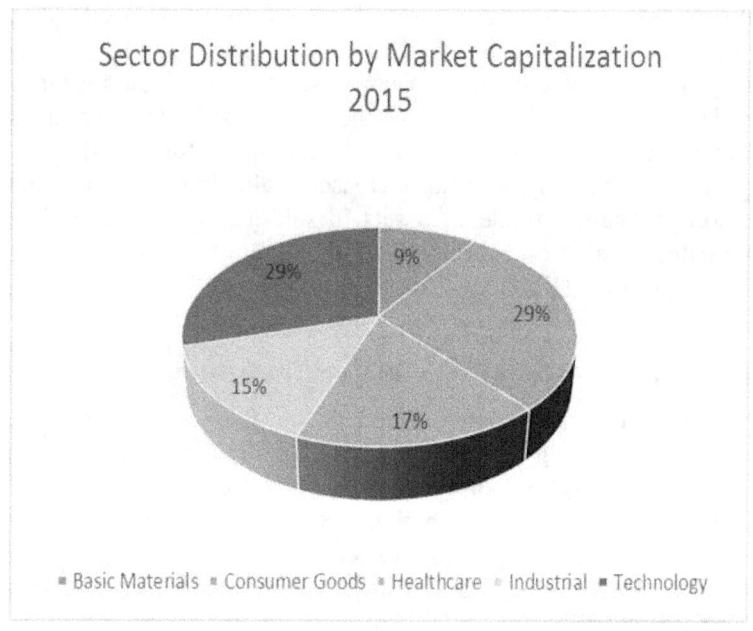

It is recognized that the consumer goods sector (29%) and healthcare (29%) together represent a disproportionate 58% of the total market capitalization, followed by technology (17%) and basic materials (9%).

Firm Identification. Primary. Due to the long-term likelihood of changes including mergers and acquisitions at which point certain names may be subsumed, the emphasis was placed on the sectors and subsectors in which the firms operate. Moreover, businesses can over time migrate from one subsector to another or straddle more than one subsector, as has been noted elsewhere. In addition, over time some subsectors may disappear in their current form in response to technological change, regulatory or other factors.

Financial Data

Source. The data are sourced from the financial statements of the selected firms in either their filings with U.S. Securities and Exchange Commission (SEC), which are typically the 20-F or 10-K Reports, or company annual reports that include the financial statements. The financial statements are generally audited by one of the "Big 4" accounting firms (formerly known as the "Big 8"), Deloitte Touche, Pricewaterhouse Coopers, Ernst&Young, and KPMG, sometimes possibly in conjunction with a local accounting office, whether or not affiliated with one of the four firms.

For non-U.S. dollar currencies, the currency units used are local and are not converted into U.S. dollars.

Stock price data were collected from online sources, such as Yahoo! Finance.

Observation Period. For the firm representing the consumer goods sector, the financial data sample covered fiscal years 1991 to 2015. For the other firms, the sample data were collected from the fiscal years from 2005 to 2015 (for firms reporting on a calendar year basis), and for the fiscal years 2006 to 2015 for firms reporting on a mid-year basis (see "Fiscal Year") below. Stock prices were obtained for the corresponding years.

Fiscal Year. For company data, the title "Year" on the horizontal axis of the chart refers to "Fiscal Year" which in most cases is calendar year as most firms report their financial information on a *calendar-year basis* i.e. for one year ending on December 31 of that year. For firms that report their financial information on a mid-year basis, the fiscal year is generally advanced by one year. For example, if ABC Inc.'s fiscal year ends on December 31st,

2015, the fiscal year is calendar year basis and is referred to as fiscal year 2015 (or abbreviated as FY 2015). If XYZ, Inc.'s fiscal year ends June 30th, 2016, XYZ's fiscal year is referred to as FY 2016.

Data Points.

RRC. The original data needed for the computation of the RRC are taken for each fiscal year are as follows. The financial statement source is indicated in bold.

Income Statement: Revenues (accrued)

Cash Flow Statement: Net cash from operations, capital expenditures, acquisitions (added to acquisitions are intangibles defined as investments).

Stock prices used were an average of two data points during each calendar year, generally February and November.

Data Transformations. The above data for each fiscal year are transformed to create new variables. RRC is calculated by dividing the cash flow return by the cash cost for the same fiscal year. Cash flow *return* is defined as NNCF and the cash cost is estimated as revenues less NNCF. For example, if NNCF is 100, and revenues is 1000, the cash cost is estimated at 900. The RRC would therefore be 100/900 or 11%. It is recognized that accrual revenues differs from cash revenues and therefore the cash cost is considered to be an estimate.

Growth rates for the RRC and stock prices are compound annual growth rates (CAGR), compounded for 3-year periods in succession. Therefore each CAGR data point represents the compound growth of the previous 3 periods; the result is that in order to produce a data point for a given year, 3 previous years of data are needed. For example, the CAGR data point for 2008 would require data for 2005, 2006 and 2007.

Alternative representation of RRC: The RRC and its growth rate can be particularly volatile; if a particular RRC growth rate is literally "off the charts" (e.g. acquisitions in 2007 for the consumer goods firm presented here resulted in a negative growth exceeding 400% in that year), then the 3-year moving average

(MA) of the RRC is used in place of the actual RRC figures, and the CAGR is calculated based on the moving average figures.

Data Discrepancies. The terminology and composition of data may differ somewhat across firms. Although the financial information is considered to be of good quality, data discrepancies can occur and the composition of certain categories such as capital expenditures may not be uniform across firms. Financial statements are always subject to revisions in subsequent years. The data used here are subject to revisions and may be updated.

RRC: RESULTS BY SECTOR

The results are presented in two sets of charts. The first set displays the individual RRC data during the sample period, along with the average and dispersion (sample standard deviation) of the data. The second set of charts, titled a *returns-to-valuation analysis*, shows the compound annual growth rates (CAGR) of both the RRC and the stock prices for each fiscal year.

Charts for each sector (and subsector where applicable) are shown below:

BASIC MATERIALS SECTOR
Oil & Gas Production

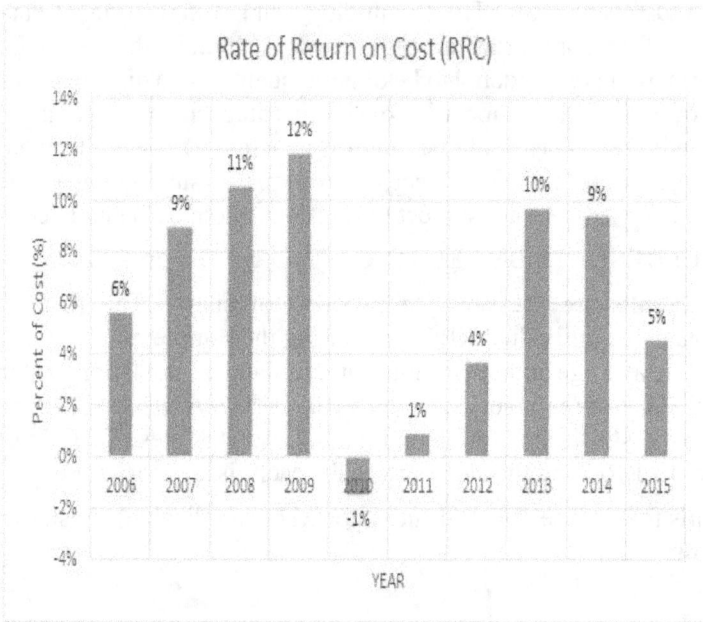

RRC
Average: 6%
Dispersion   4%

*Dispersion refers to the sample standard deviation; normality assumption may not be valid.

*Data to June 2015

Integrated Oil Companies

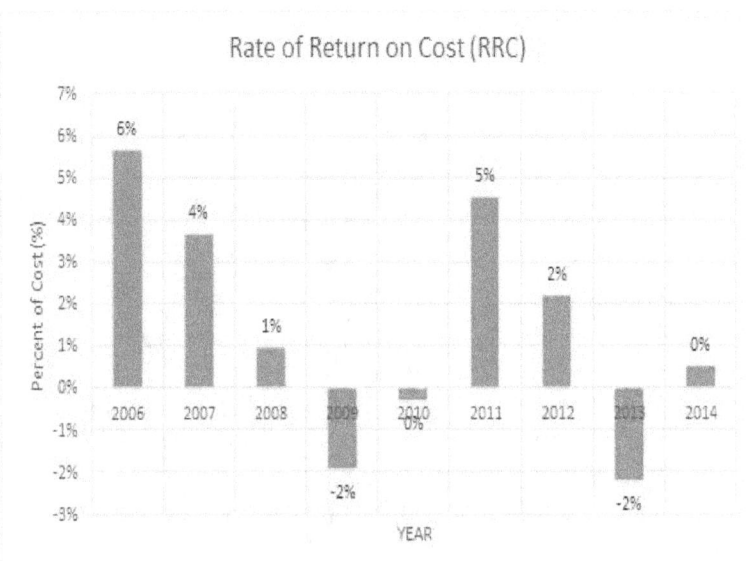

RRC

Average: 1%

Dispersion 3%

Dispersion refers to the sample standard deviation; normality assumption may not be valid.

CONSUMER GOODS SECTOR

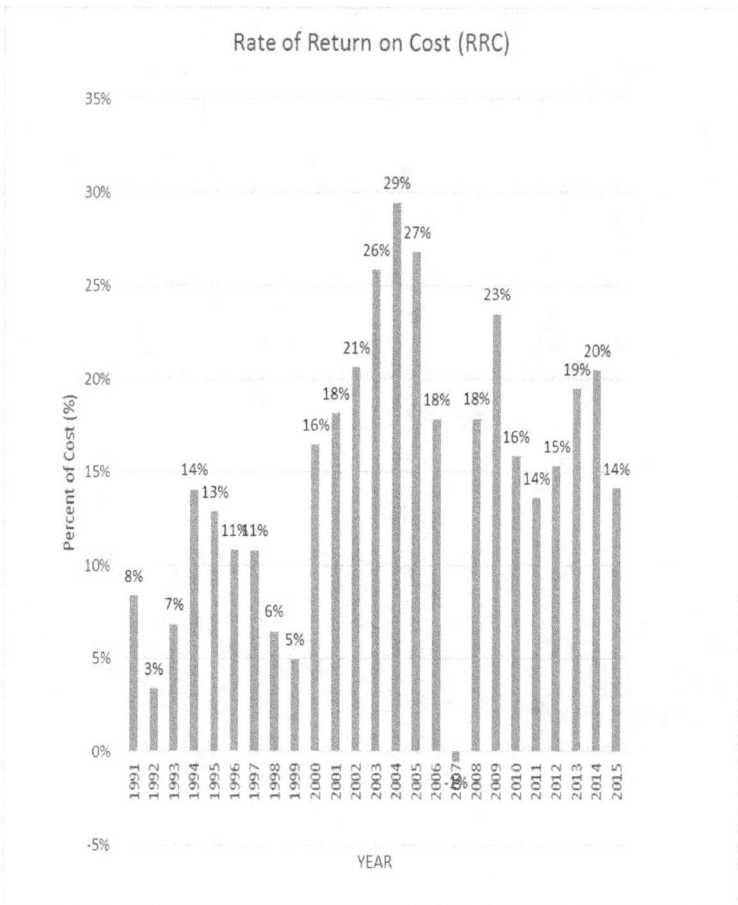

RRC (based on expanded sample, fiscal years 1991-2015)
Average: 15%
Dispersion: 7.5%

HEALTHCARE SECTOR

Rate of Return on Cost (RRC)

RRC
Average: 18%
Dispersion 14%

*Dispersion refers to the sample standard deviation; normality assumption may not be valid.

INDUSTRIAL GOODS SECTOR

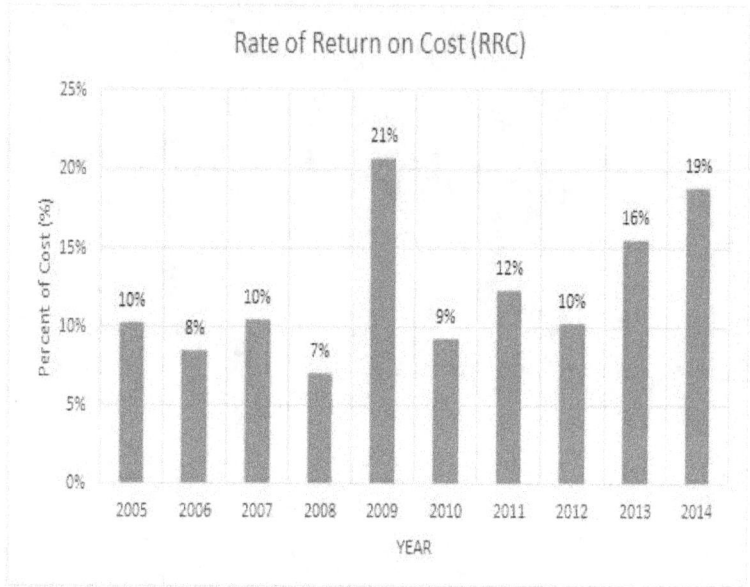

RRC

Average: 12%

Dispersion 5%

Dispersion refers to the sample standard deviation; normality assumption may not be valid.

TECHNOLOGY SECTOR

Semiconductors-Integrated circuits

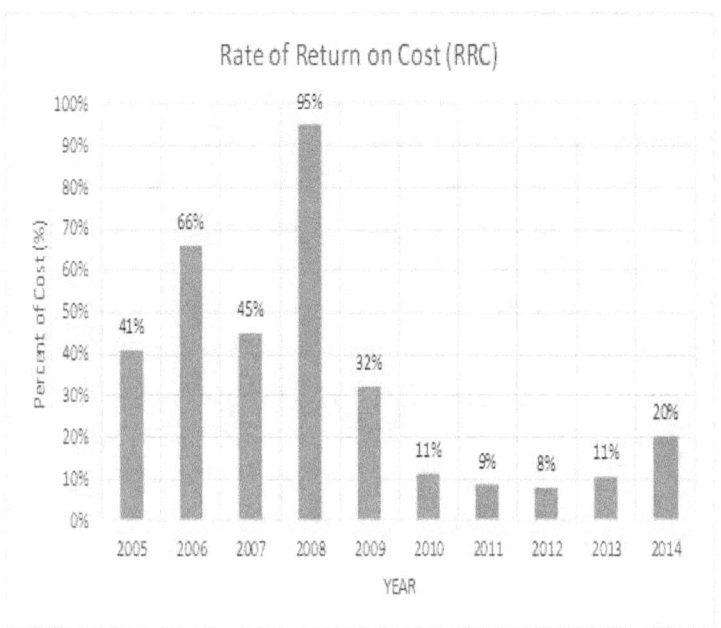

RRC

Average:	34%
Dispersion	29%

*Dispersion refers to the sample standard deviation; normality assumption may not be valid.

Communications equipment

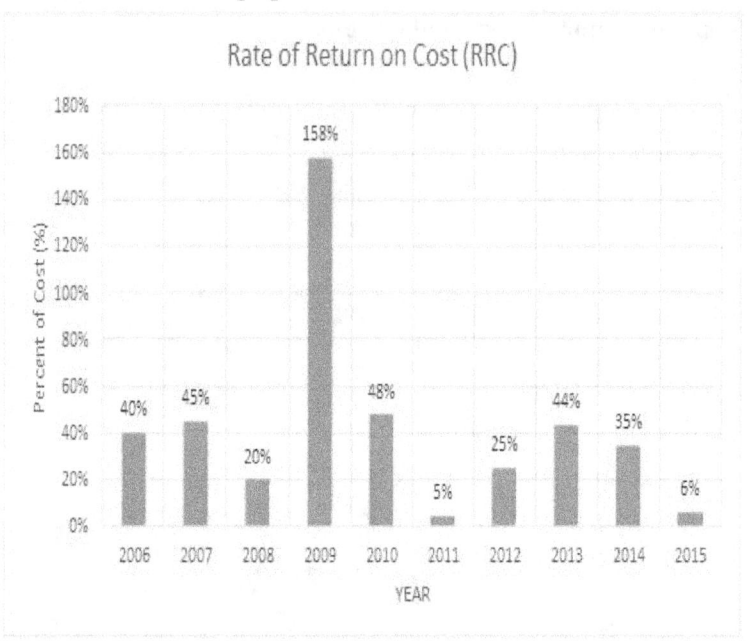

Rate of Return on Cost (RRC)

RRC
Average: 43%
Dispersion   43%

Dispersion refers to the sample standard deviation; normality assumption may not be valid.

*Data to September 2015.

COMPARING THE NNCF RATIO TO THE RRC

Briefly, for purposes of comparison the NNCF Ratio is charted alongside the rate of return on cost (RRC) for the fiscal years 1991 to 2015. Recall that the NNCF is *NCF adjusted for the cost of acquisitions and other items* as explained above, and can also be referred to as the *return, net benefit* and as the firm's *equity income.* The NNCF ratio is *NNCF/Revenues* of the firm. The data is for the same consumer goods firm as shown above; the data for the RRC is transformed from a bar graph to a line graph. (Note that at the bottom left of the chart the NNCF ratio is mislabeled as the NCF ratio).

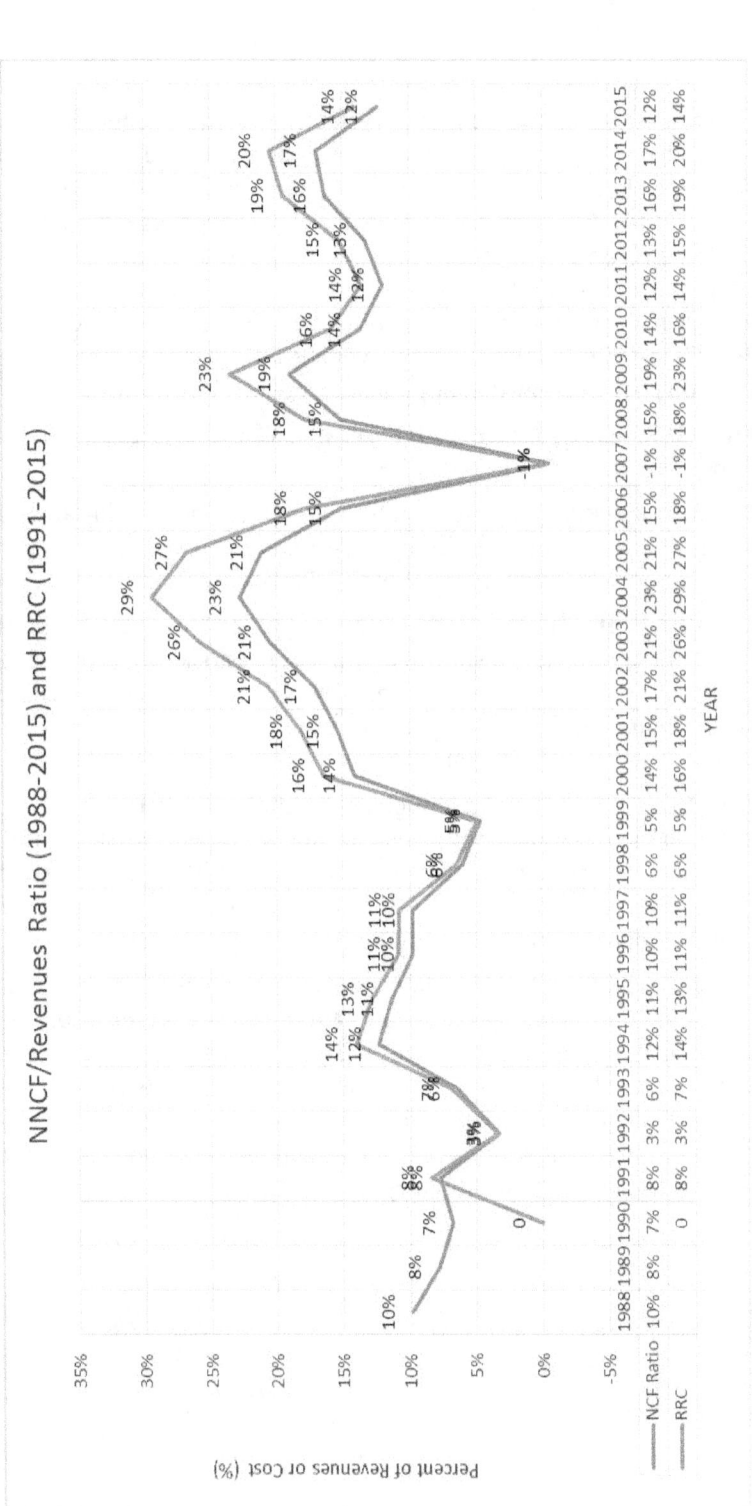

NNCF/Revenues Ratio (1988-2015) and RRC (1991-2015)

	1988	1989	1990	1991	1992	1993	1994	1995	1996	1997	1998	1999	2000	2001	2002	2003	2004	2005	2006	2007	2008	2009	2010	2011	2012	2013	2014	2015
NCF Ratio	10%	8%	7%	8%	3%	6%	12%	11%	10%	6%	5%	14%	15%	17%	21%	23%	21%	15%	-1%	18%	19%	14%	12%	13%	16%	17%	12%
RRC			0	8%	3%	7%	14%	13%	11%	6%	5%	16%	18%	21%	26%	29%	27%	18%	-1%	15%	23%	16%	14%	15%	19%	20%	14%

A correlation between the two variables is visually apparent. For the period 1991-2015, the means (averages) for the NNCF ratio and the RRC are 12% and 15%, respectively; the standard deviation is 6%, and 7.5%, respectively. This suggests that the RRC is a somewhat more volatile measure historically. RRC is expected to be higher than the NNCF ratio because the RRC divides the NNCF by *cost*, while the NNCF ratio divides the NNCF by (the usually greater) revenues figure; the exception is in fiscal years when NNCF approaches zero.

RETURNS-TO-VALUATION ANALYSIS: APPLICATION OF THE RRC TO EQUITIES

Growth in asset values is not aligned with the growth in rates of return, suggests the possibility of a *rates of return-to-valuation gap* (abbreviated as *returns-to-valuation* gap).

Asset Mispricing. Any "gap" appearing between the two lines indicates either a possible overvaluation (stock price growing faster than the RRC)—represented by a black bar, or a possible undervaluation (the RRC growing faster than the stock price)—represented by a white bar.

The "gaps" are viewed as rough approximations, and it should be emphasized that a single year is not sufficient to determine whether overvaluation (undervaluation) exists; a persistent *returns-to-valuation gap* of say 3 or more years provides more solid evidence of asset mispricing.

Where the RRC growth data is particularly volatile, the returns-to-valuation charts present the alternative representation as explained above of RRC using a 3-year *moving average* of the RRC data. This was the case for the consumer goods firm which had an outsized cost item (acquisitions) in one year during the sample. Due to the quality of reproduction of the images, some details may be somewhat blurry.

BASIC MATERIALS
Oil & Gas Production

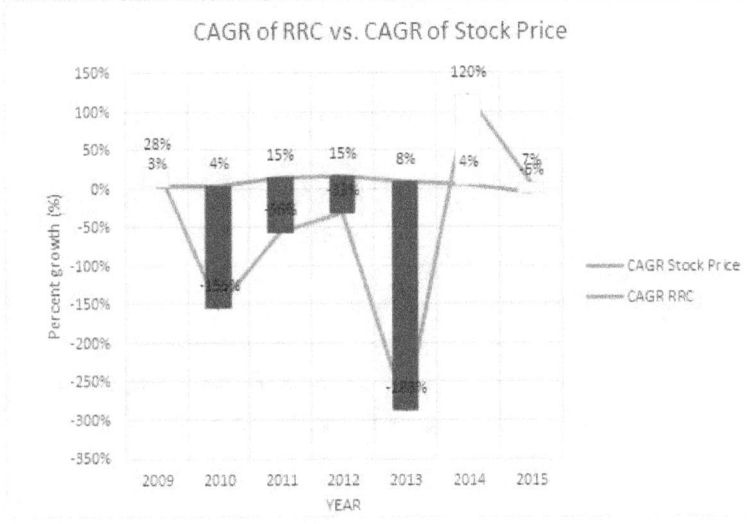

CAGR refers to the compound annual growth rate.

Integrated Oil

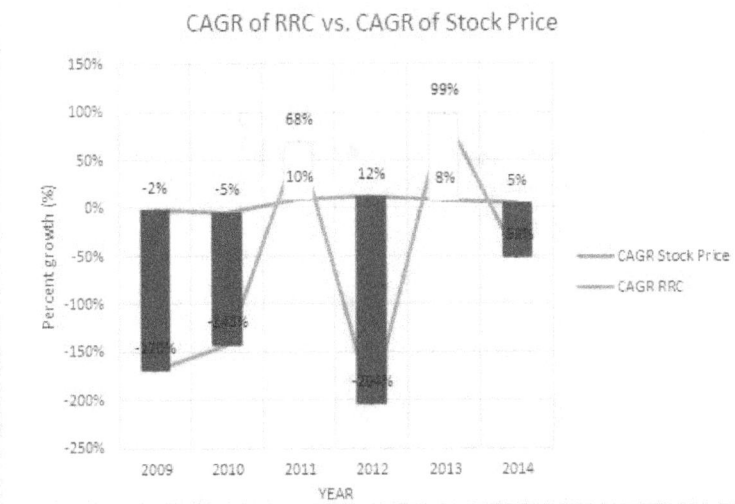

CAGR refers to the compound annual growth rate.

CONSUMER GOODS

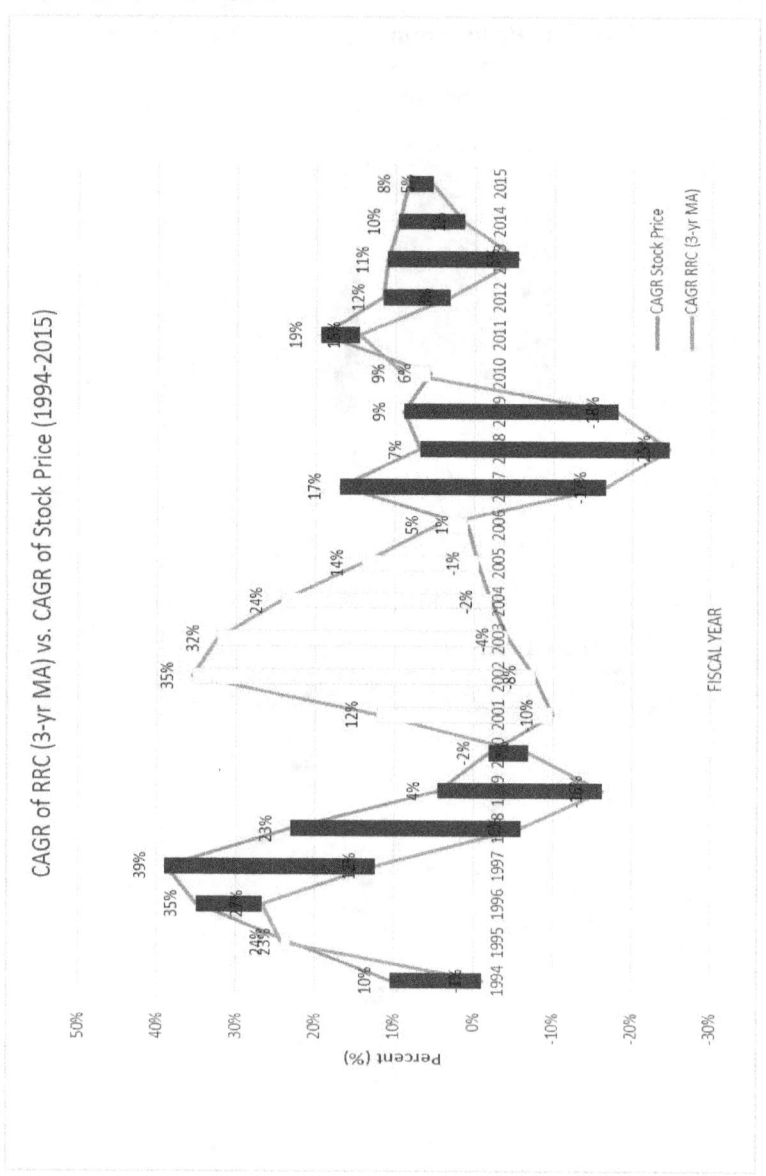

*Based on expanded sample: Fiscal years 1994-2015 (to Dec 31).

HEALTHCARE

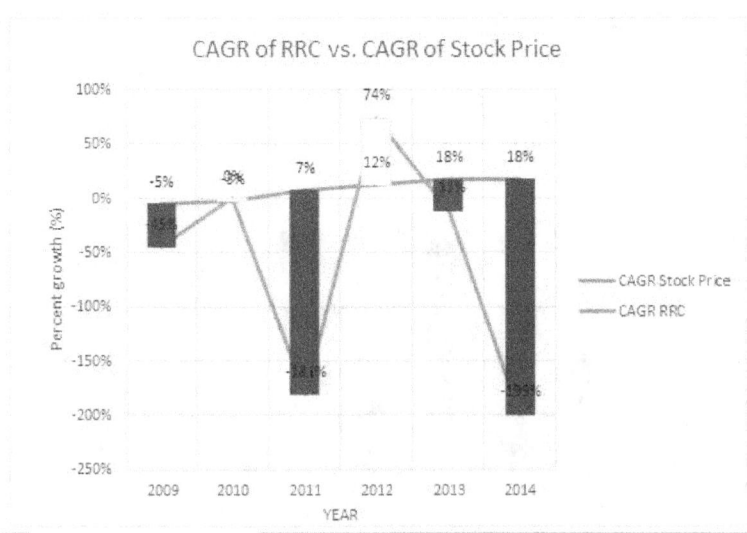

INDUSTRIAL GOODS

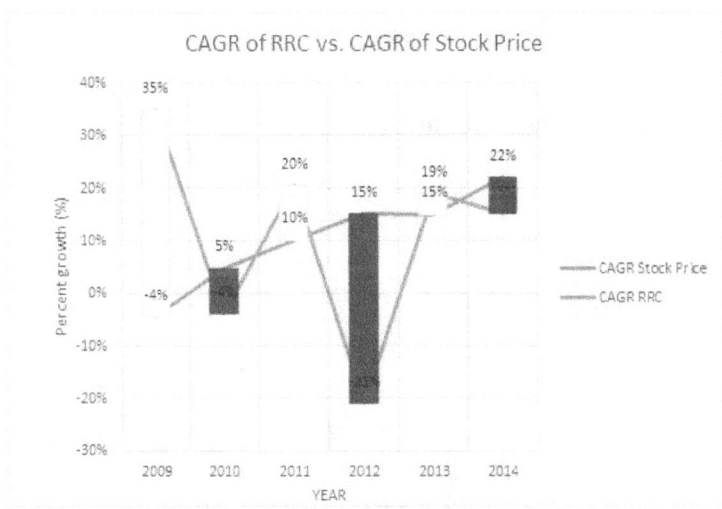

CAGR refers to the compound annual growth rate.

TECHNOLOGY

Semiconductors-Integrated Circuits

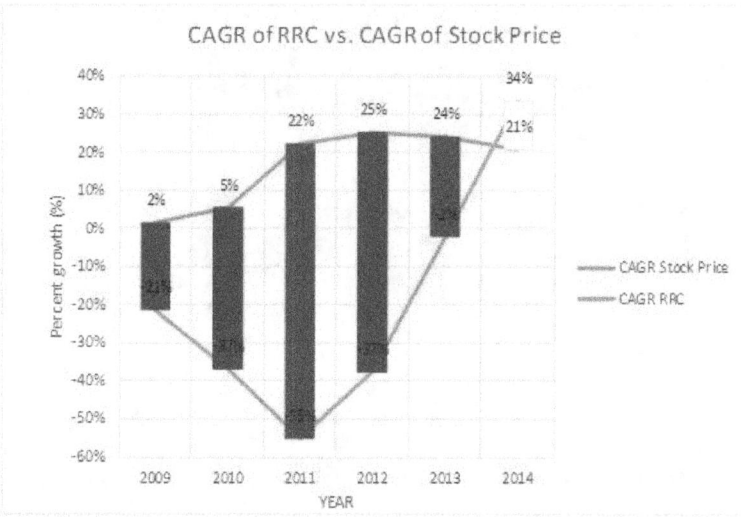

CAGR refers to the compound annual growth rate.

Communications Equipment

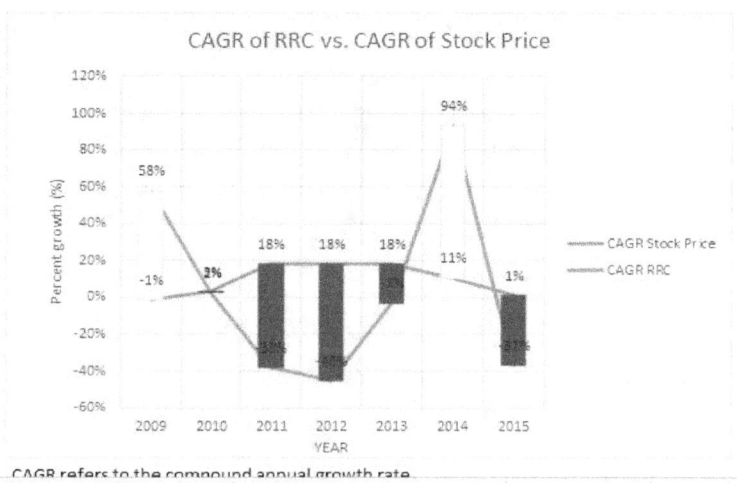

CAGR refers to the compound annual growth rate.

CATEGORY #1B: FINANCIAL ENTITIES (INDIVIDUALS)

Rate of Return on Cost of Living (RRCOL). Beyond its application to asset pricing, the concept of rates of return to cost (RRC) (or abbreviated as returns-to-cost) may apply to individuals as well (Category #1B from the framework table). Rates of return (using cost of living, abbreviated COL) can help individuals decide whether a particular place to live and work is to their *net* benefit or not (it is key to note "net" means net of costs of living; if at some point location becomes irrelevant to employment (i.e. remote employment), cost of living may still be a factor in decision-making as to where one wishes to live.

Recall the rate of return relationship as presented earlier in the context of a financial entity (organization/business):

Net benefit/Cost

Where the *net benefit* =gross revenues less the associated cost. In the case of the *cost of living*, the wording changes to:

Net (Amount) Saved/Cost of living

To avoid confusion, "net (amount) saved" is not the same as "savings." The net amount saved is a net flow of income during the period: The individual earned 100 currency units in the year, had expenditures throughout the year of 98 currency units, with the difference of 100-98 or 2 currency units saved. This amount saved can be now added to any accumulated "savings" which is defined as a balance sheet item (or "stock" as opposed to "flow"): So, for example, the individual has 50 currency units in his/her bank account, then the additional "saved" currency units can be added to the 50, for a new total savings balance of 52 currency units.

Although for both businesses and indviduals a *net benefit* is involved we use different language: For businesses we say "net profit" or "net cash flow" while for individuals and households we refer to "savings."

Stigler (1987) discusses cost of living in the context of utility theory. He qualifies the term cost of living to mean *consumer expenditures*, "…the cost over time or between places, of living at a constant level – which means, of course, staying on the same indifference curve." In reference to cost of living indices, he asks

106

in which year a family would have been better off if it earned $20,000 in 1980 and $25,000 in 1985. We cannot know the answer until we have an idea of their cost of living. Stigler states " The answer is that if a (perfect*) index of the cost of living rose less than 25 percent between these years, the family was "better off" in 1985." He clarifies that a perfect index "…would take account of income taxes and public subsidies and services." (Stigler: 67)

Extending this exercise, a rate of return relationship can be posited. For example, in 1980 the cost of living index is 100 and the annual household income of the family is $20,000. Assuming that nothing was saved by the family in 1980 meaning that their expenditures were equal to their income, then their rate of return was 0 or (0/20000) By 1985, the cost of living index has risen by 20% (less than their income which has risen by 25%), so that their costs would be 24,000. Recall that the family earned 25,000 in 1985, so that now a net benefit after living costs (=savings) of 1000 have emerged. The rate of return relationship can be shown as follows for each year:

1980:   RR=0/20000 or 0%

1985:   RR=1000/25000 or 4%

The 1985 rate of return for this family suggests that the family is better off from a *rate of return on cost of living* standpoint. Although such rate of return figures may not be readily available for various cities (metropolitan statistical areas), etc., such information may become more readily available over time. It might become possible for individuals with limited means to identify where they could improve their financial condition based on their skill set and income-earning potential. It should be clarified that the income-earning potential in this case is likely *wage income* or salary.

Income and RRCOL Disparity. While income in the form of high salaries/wages may attract labor, there may be pitfalls to focusing on income alone. If high wages are offered in an area with high cost of living, then people moving in search of better wages and living conditions may unknowingly find themselves in a worse situation than before. For example, a worker living in Town A where the rate of return on cost of living is near zero (i.e. breakeven income to expenditures), sees higher wages being offered in Town B and decides to move to town B in search of a better life. However, even though the wages in Town B may be higher, if the rate of return on the cost of living there is negative, then the worker is in a worse position than before.

Thus, looking at income alone may be insufficient information to make the decision: Areas with rising wages/salaries in combination with falling costs of living (i.e. higher rates of return on cost of living) and may suggest better prospects for increased net income.

It is understood that looking only at rates of return on cost of living is an oversimplification because there may be other reasons why one might be willing to accept a low (or negative) rate of return. Decisions are made by individuals according to their own, subjective valuation; therefore, while a rate of return on living cost might be very low, the individual may highly value living there for other reasons (family, friends, activities, local environment, etc.). In addition, rates of return could be expected to vary significantly for different people in the same geographic area; for example, due to similar preferences and tastes while they may choose to live in a similar residential zone with similar costs, but one may be have a higher income than the other, and therefore a higher rate of return on cost of living. Tastes and preferences are an important factor in the rate of return calculus; two individuals with identical incomes may have significantly different rates of return on cost of living because one has so-called "expensive" tastes while the other lives very frugally.

Price Deflation and Increased Purchasing Power. In the previous example, the worker's rate of return on cost of living in Town B was initially zero, and no raises (increased income/wages) were offered. Suppose that during the year the cost of living declines by 3%. While wages never rose, *the rate of return on living costs* has risen, simply by virtue of the decline in living costs rather than increased wage income. For example, if the cost of living was 100 currency units per year and the person saves nothing during the entire year, the rate of return on the cost of living is 0%, or:

$$(100-100)/100=0\%$$

With 3% consumer price deflation over the year, no change in consumption patterns and income unchanged at 100 currency units per year, the rate of return on his/her cost of living is about 3.1%, or:

$$(100-97)/97=3.1\%$$

It could be argued that consumption patterns and habits change all the time and therefore such an example is not relevant. However, it is a rough guide to what can happen when consumer prices trend downwards over time while incomes do not rise.

Debt Bias and Deflation. In contrast to the purchasing power benefits of consumer price deflation, it is recognized that deflation, specifically *producer price* and *asset deflation* can have significant adverse impacts in economies with a debt bias (i.e. heavily reliant upon debt). Producer price *deflation* impacts indebted businesses as the prices of their goods and services (and revenues) fall, resulting in less cash flow to service their debts without cutting their expenses. Individuals and businesses who have borrowed heavily against assets that *deflate* in value can find themselves in a *negative equity position;* this means that in order to sell /liquidate the asset additional cash would need to be raised to repay the principal balance of the loan. It could also be added that in deflations governments may also experience declines in nominal tax revenues and therefore encounter difficulty in repaying their (nominal) obligations. Although the deflation itself is often blamed as the source of the problem, it could be argued that *over-indebtedness* is the primary source of the problem. Tools to better evaluate debt service capacity (DSC) are discussed in Kennedy (2015) and revisited briefly in the Appendix.

Summary of Income Sources

Although the discussion above on income was limited to salary/wages, it should be pointed out that there are potentially multiple sources of income for individuals that when combined constitute their total income. Savings through increased purchasing power gained by lower costs of certain goods is also potentially significant, but may often be overlooked as a source of "income." It is acknowledged that modern economies may tend to have an inflationary, rather than a deflationary, bias with respect to certain consumer goods, while technological advances and cost efficiencies have led to substantial cost reductions for other goods originating from the communications and information technology industries.

A general list of possible income sources of individuals as financial entities is shown below, conforming to the categories of the framework table in Part I (with the exception of wage/salary income which does not appear in the framework table):

Wage/Salary, from employer or; linking to category #2B-- employer as one's *own* business/ (asset as financial entity-organization).

Price deflation increasing *purchasing power* of wage/salary income over time.

#2 **Assets owned**: Business, farm, real estate, websites, rights*:
> Distributions/Draws (in addition to salary/wage above)

#3 **Assets as Capital of a financial entity. Debt and Equity.**
> Interest Income*, Dividend/Distributions/Draws

#4 **Other Assets. Reliance on Future Purchasing Power:**
> Capital gains on asset sales.
> Price deflation increasing purchasing power of cash/currency.

Notes and Additional Commentary

Rights. Income deriving from a form of asset broadly called "rights" owned by an individual could include royalty income, income from copyrights and trademarks, share of revenues from "virtual" real estate such as revenue-generating websites, etc. Legal definitions and distinctions may exist.

Interest Income (Category #3B, #4A). In addition to interest received from debt securities such as bonds (capital of a financial entity) historically interest from bank deposits has existed. The question might arise where interest income from cash deposited in bank savings accounts would appear in the list above, although in the low interest rate / low return environment of the early 21st century it is hard to conceive of much current income being derived from bank savings (and even securities to some extent). With regards to bank savings accounts (deposits), which in the 20th century were known to pay significant interest during certain periods, such assets could be thought of indirectly as a form of "lending" via the banking institution, or Category #3B. However, if the deposit pays no interest, then Category #4A could apply. If the deposit is a form of bailment, then *fees* may apply; in a *negative interest rate* environment, lenders and depositors may be charged for holding their deposits in a bank account or owning bonds.

If no interest is paid on cash deposits, then the only source of "income" would be from *price deflation* increasing the purchasing power of the cash holdings over time over and above the fees charged.

Transfer Payments. The question might arise whether transfer payments, such as various types of social welfare benefits, public and needy family assistance, child tax credits and other forms of income that originate from another source should be included in the total of income. For a proper accounting, it would seem best to have a total figure that excludes transfer payments and then a separate figure for the amount of transfer payments so as to ascertain how much income is being provided from outside sources (akin to a "financing source" in a business sense). It is recognized that some transfer payments are not necessarily public assistance-related, and that there can be private transfer payments from other family members or churches, etc. Therefore, the data could be divided into *total income generated by the individual* (including from assets owned by the individual according to the framework table), *income from public assistance*, and *income from private* sources (e.g. family, church assistance).

Policy Impacts on the RRCOL. In the current economic environment of the 21st century, we are faced with low (policy) interest rates that tend to affect Category #3 and Category #4, since certain assets appreciate in value in function of the lowering of policy interest rates (e.g. securities). In an environment with an inflationary debt bias (even at low inflation rates of 2%), price deflation no longer factors into the increased purchasing power (real) income of wages/salary or holdings of cash/currency. These elements should not be overlooked when considering rates of return on the cost of living (RRCOL), since opportunities for benefiting from greater rates of return may have been stymied by the policy environment.

Rates of return on COL and Income Inequality. The subject of income inequality remains a topic of much debate and relevance in political discourse. Richard Cantillon, mentioned previously as a co-founder of economics along with Adam Smith, should also be credited with a remarkable observation on monetary origins of inflation and *income redistribution*: When the quantity of money expands (as opposed to being fixed), a redistribution of income may occur through a time lag between those who benefit from the rise of prices and incomes *first* and those who experience them later. Geographic disparities in income and prices may also occur as debt is repaid and the money flows from one area to another. Nearly two centuries later, Ludwig von Mises (re: Austrian school of economics) revived Cantillon's observations on price differentials (Heimann: 43) in his landmark *Theory of Money and Credit* (1912).

The implication is that those who receive new debt-money from the banking system as part of the lending process (aka, credit creation) have greater purchasing power than others as prices have not yet risen uniformly.

This point raises an important question regarding income inequality – In addition to comparing income inequality, it may also be useful and in some cases more informative to compare inequality of rates of return on the cost of living of individuals (as well as the RRC for businesses and other financial entities).

It is recognized that the research on purchasing power parity (PPP) already attempts to provide information in order to better compare individuals' relative cost of living across countries. With the RRCOL, it may also be possible to compare individuals in markedly different environments and countries. For example, if the RRCOL in City A and City B are estimated at 5%, and 0%, respectively, then those in City B could be viewed as less well-off.

Returns-to-Consumer Price Gap for RRCOL: Policy Implications

Poverty Prevention. Analogous to the *returns-to-valuation analysis* above for income real estate and equities, it is possible to apply a *returns-to-consumer price gap*: Consumer price growth would be expected to approximately align with the growth in "personal*" rate of return on the cost of living* (RRCOL) of

112

individuals. The analysis could be useful as a monitoring tool to fight poverty: If consumer price growth consistently exceeds the growth in the RRCOL there might be an argument that the policy environment has an inflationary bias that hurts the real purchasing power of individuals, a significant cause of poverty.

Concluding Remarks: A Theory of Returns-to-Pricing?

In the context of income real estate valuation and capitalization rates of Part I, a theorized relationship between rates of return and pricing of assets began to emerge as an alternative to net income (NOI) and pricing. Subsequently in Part I and then in depth in Part II, a relationship between rates of return and the pricing of equities was explored, as an alternative to relating net income (EPS) to pricing. Beyond asset markets, the logic was applied to individuals as financial entities whose cost is the *cost of living*, and who may generate a "net benefit" (return) in the form of net saved income.

When we attempt to price something according to its "true" or "fundamental" value, what are the sources of this "value"? It is theorized that rates of return on financial entities, specifically rates of return on cost (RRC), are a fundamental *point of reference* for the rates of return on *assets*, as well as a fundamental driver of value as a guide in pricing. Recall that "rates" are often referred to in the plural form since there are presumed to be potentially countless rates of return in an economy. This in no way suggests that rates of return and values should "line up" perfectly, only that in theory --and absent external policy interventions-- there could be a central tendency, such that fundamental value tends to derive from rates of return—beginning with rates of return on financial entities.

The concept of *subjective value*, as touched upon in the text, should not be excluded from the analysis of value as subjective value is also considered integral to the process of valuation, alongside rates of return.

Analytically, the relationship may be best monitored by *growth* in prices relative to *growth* in rates of return over time. It is acknowledged that volatility of rates of return can pose problems for analysis, and therefore longer periods of historical data and moving averages may help normalize the figures somewhat. Price growth that exceeds the growth in the rate of return (on cost or cost of living) is theorized to result in an unsustainable "disconnect" or "gap", with possible consequences in asset marked "crashes" as well as the impoverishment of individuals.

This returns-to-pricing relationship in its most general form--encompassing both assets and goods markets--is summarized as follows:

$$\Delta P \cong \Delta r$$

...where P is the change (or growth) in *pricing* (or *valuation*) of a given asset or good, and r is the rate of return of financial entities—to reiterate, financial entity rates of return are only a viewed as a *point of reference*. For example, for Category #1A financial entities (organizations/firms), P would be the pricing of the equities, and r is the rate of return on cost (RRC) of the firm.

For Category #1B financial entities as individuals, P is the pricing of consumption goods and services, and r is the rate of return on cost of living (RRCOL). The question might arise how consumption goods can be "priced" since they are not assets and are not evaluated in the same way. It is probable that the pricing of goods and services originates from various interrelated phenomena: From *consumers* based on their own financial situations (as roughly represented by their rate of return on cost of living), their subjective values, the decisions* of *producers* of the goods and providers of services*, and finally by *policy* interventions (regulatory, fiscal, monetary) that can cause re-pricing of goods and services.

these decisions could include decisions to stop or reduce production if required rates of return are not being realized on those products.

Because economies have historically been subject to multiple interventions, whether regulatory, fiscal or monetary, empirical research using time series data may not readily reveal a returns-valuation relationship. Nevertheless, future research could help provide additional evidence. In the meantime, as a monitoring tool returns-valuation analysis can possibly serve as an additional resource to anticipate any emergent "disconnects" and perhaps correct for them. A summary of analytical tools is provided in Appendix 7, Policy Directions.

APPENDICES

CONTENTS

APPENDIX 1

ECONOMIC ENTITIES AND ECONOMIC ACTIVITY

This book centers on financial entities and the *financial* element of rates of return analysis. A distinction between financial and economic entities was not made in Kennedy (2015). The economic entity concept and its components are introduced here as a rough sketch.

Voluntary Activity. Although often overlooked, a basic concept to begin with of the term "economic" would be that a financial entity is roughly able to support itself from *voluntary* activity which includes revenues, costs and financing activity. Activity that is not voluntary is not viewed as economic [Walker (1888):

115

5]   From a strictly financial viewpoint, while an entity could function and achieve a net surplus financially from its productive activities, but could be engaging in involuntary activity that includes the violation of human rights through forced labor or conscription, or legally-imposed sales that result from compulsion (i.e. customers are required by law to purchase the good or service). Additional examples might be laws/legal requirements, including those that fix the price(s) of certain *inputs* so as to improve the profitability of *other* financial entities that use the inputs. Examples of involuntary means may be numerous and exceedingly complex; monetary dynamics may also be considered.

Financially Unsustainable Entities. Many entities may be financially unsustainable, unable to consistently cover their costs from their revenues/sales (including revenues as outside donations or proceeds from fund drives for non-profits), yet still be considered economic in the sense of being supported by *voluntary* financing sources. There may be various *personal reasons* why individuals or groups might be willing to continue engaging in the activity voluntarily, reflecting their *subjective values* [re: Carl Menger, William Stanley Jevons, and Leon Walras on the subject of imputation of value; Menger (1871)]. In such cases, additional voluntary contributions from members/organizers might be needed to keep the operations running—i.e. *voluntary* financing activity. This might describe certain organizations such as non-profits (NPOs) and non-governmental organizations (NGOs).

Financially unsustainable entities may not be economic in the sense that their financing sources could be considered entirely voluntary; combined with a political element, the finances of many governments are typically under pressure from various special interests to increase spending without counterbalancing special interests to restrain spending. The result is that expenditures of these entities may tend to consistently rise faster than revenues, leading to a constant need for outside financing sources; prolonged economic downturns (including deflationary depressions) can result in eventual default and even bankruptcy.

Christ (1968, 1979) accounts for the sources of government financing to cover the costs of their activities: *Taxes*, *bonds* and *high-powered money* (also called *base money*). Taxes involve the removal of income flows from one part of the economy to put elsewhere according to various political priorities. Government bonds are issued to borrow from the public or other entities, including financial institutions and central banks. The central bank can produce high-powered money by purchasing assets, most notably government bonds. *New* issues of government bonds may arise when government expenditures exceed tax revenues (resulting in *deficits*) in a given time period. There is a potential international dimension to the sources of financing. This includes high-powered money financing by foreign central banks. Using an example of the U.S., a foreign central bank can purchase U.S. government bonds (Treasuries) as part of their currency policies, which provides a source of financing to the U.S. government that does not necessitate the creation of high-powered money by the monetary authority of the U.S (i.e. the Federal Reserve); the high-powered money creation rests with the foreign countries in their currencies.

Consequences. A concern is the economy-wide consequence of such financially unsustainable entities requiring the above financing sources, each of which may have negative economic impacts to varying degrees: This can include disincentives to produce due to possibly punitive marginal tax rates, over-indebtedness due to artificially lowered interest rates, price inflation due to money creation (causing potential hardship for individuals on fixed incomes, even at moderately low but sustained inflation), or debt-based monetary *deflation* during a credit crunch when over-indebtedness causes systemic banking seize-ups and lending contraction through fractional reserve banking. The net effect over long periods of time of these consequences can be unsustainable debt accumulation coupled with lower overall incomes to service the debt—the opposite of desirable policy objectives, as well as detrimental to economic viability and sustainability.

Debt Accumulation: Detail

The obligations that governments have accumulated over the 20th and early 21st century, which includes the unfunded liabilities for pension and health care systems, have become unsustainable. . Economist Lawrence Kotlikoff of Boston University testified that the United States' *fiscal gap* stands at US$210 trillion, or some 16 times greater than the official U.S. debt figure. (Hollingsworth 2015). The problem of "peak debt" has been raised by Stockman (2013, 2016). Other recent analyses of public debt and fiscal problems are found in Alesina and Giavazzi, Eds. (2013).

Negative Interest Rates (Yields). In order to further reduce borrowing costs for unsustainable financial entities, *negative interest rates* (yields on bonds) have now become a feature of debt markets. As of early 2016, some $US 7 trillion of government debt worldwide currently trades at negative rates; the average yield on the Bank of America Merrill Lynch World Sovereign Bond Index at 1.29%. (McCormick 2016)

Explanatory Notes

Definitions of terms may vary depending upon the study and presentation of data. An important distinction must be made between official government debt figures and the fiscal gap figures. Note for example that the McKinsey Global Institute (2015) report focuses primarily on official debt figures. See below for further clarification.

Debt-to-GDP Ratio. Various measures exist and include:

(1) Debt owed by households, nonfinancial corporations and governments
(2) Households, corporate, government and financial debt outstanding
(3) Official government debt figures (=cash basis accounting)
(4) Specifically when referring to the *fiscal gap**, debt includes the *unfunded liabilities* (e.g. liabilities of the pension/Social Security and Medicare systems of the U.S. Federal government).
*Fiscal Gap. Defined by Kotlikoff as "the difference between our government's projected financial obligations and the present value of all projected future tax and other receipts." (Hollingsworth, 2015). For purposes of comparison, the U.S. official government debt is approximately $13T or 74% of the GDP of the U.S., while the fiscal gap is an estimated $210T.

The IMF estimates the U.S. fiscal gap at 14% of the present discounted value of U.S. GDP; this 14% figure measures the *adjustment needed* so that the present value of the excess of future expenditure and current liabilities over future receipts is zero, over an infinite horizon. In the 3% discount rate scenario, closing the fiscal gap would require a "permanent annual fiscal adjustment equal to about 14 percent of U.S. GDP..."(IMF 2010 53:54).

APPENDIX 2

Public Investment in the 20th Century: An Assessment

Models and Public Investment Policy. During the 20th century and through to the present, growth and output models [re: Cobb-Douglas (1928)] and the GDP *national income accounting* framework may have been used as justifications for public investment, including infrastructure spending. The stated objective is to stimulate economic development and growth, however growth may be defined.

In many cases infrastructure spending is an integral element of the development process. However, as Bauer (1984) notes: "(M)uch of capital formation is not a pre-condition of material advance but its concomitant.....Much of the so-called infrastructure (roads, railways and the like) is also a collection of assets and facilities which do not precede or determine development, but are largely developed in the course of it." (Bauer: 248)

The 20th Century Record. A concern rises when capital formation tends to consist of so-called "roads" or "bridges to nowhere:" Bauer provides examples: "...much public spending routinely termed investment has nothing to do with productive* capital formation. Familiar examples include prestige projects of all kinds, the creation of brand new capital cities, collectivized villages, military barracks or political prisons or the establishment of expensive and uneconomic domestic capital goods industries." (249)

It is worth pointing out the body of research on problems of policy-induced capital investment economic development of the 20th century. Bauer cites a number of studies on the historical record of public investment policy (Abramovitz 1956, Cairncross

1962, Denison 1974, Kuznets 1966, Solow 1957), and cites Kuznets: "While various modifications can be introduced into this statistical allocation, and while the results clearly vary among individual countries, the inescapable conclusion is that the direct contribution of man-hours and capital accumulation would hardly account for more than a tenth of the rate of growth in per capital product – and probably less." (Kuznets, 1966: 80-81 as cited by Bauer: 242). According to Kuznets, the remaining ninety percent or more of the increase in the rate of growth would be attributable to increased *efficiency* of productive* resources (defined as a rise in *output* per unit of input), due to one or all of the following factors: Improved resource quality, effects of changing arrangements, and impact of technological change.

*Note: The economics literature may tend to emphasize *productivity* (greater output per unit of input) rather than rates of return in a financial sense. Examination of rates of return on projects can also serve to illustrate how investment expenditures may be unjustified and uneconomic: Since the funds for such expenditures are typically furnished from taxpayer resources, it could be argued that the taxpayers could have received better rates of return on their funds elsewhere, and the increased returns would have been able to provide greater economic stimulus.

APPENDIX 3
Rates of Return as Drivers of Interest Rates: A History

The subject of rates of return and their relationship to interest rates is revisited here. This section begins with the *classical* view dominant in the 17th to roughly the early 20th century. A transformation appears to have occurred in the 20th century that resulted in a critical element of the classical view--the so-called *interest rate gap*--essentially disappearing from mainstream discourse. This interesting historical phenomenon is detailed below

In the classical view, interest was viewed as deriving from some measure of profit, with some differences of opinion as to the degree. Wicksell's *natural interest rate* (Wicksell 1898) was also viewed as a "portion of the rate of profits" in classical political

120

economy (Panico: 195). Commentary by John Locke, Adam Smith and David Ricardo on this matter are provided below.

A reference to returns by John Locke (1668) concerns the impact of a legal interest rate cap on the distribution of profits between merchant and lender. Prior to the law, the merchant and the lender (userer) the profits were split 50-50, half as profit to the merchant and half as interest to the lender. Locke argues that the law will favor the merchant: "...for if he borrow at 4 per cent and his returns be 12 per cent, he will have 8 per cent and the userer (lender) 4, whereas they divide it now equally at 6 percent." (Hutchison 1988: 63)

Adam Smith (1776) perhaps best clarified the relationship between the interest rate and profit: "The interest of money is always a derivative revenue, which if it is not paid from the profit which is made by the use of the money, must be paid from some other source of revenue, unless the borrower is a spendthrift, who contracts a second debt in order to pay the interest of the first." (46)

On the above point, credit should be given to a predecessor of Smith, Richard Cantillon (1680-1734), whose posthumously published work in 1755 *Essai sur la Nature du Commerce en Général (1755)* addresses the nature of the rate of interest. Heimann (1964) states: "There is no doubt that the nearest rival to Smith—not to Quesnay—for the honor of being the co-founder of economics is Cantillon...." (Heimann: 44). On the origin of interest, Cantillon is cited as follows ("it" refers to interest): "But its constant practice in states appears to be founded on the profits which Entrepreneurs can make out of it." (Heimann: 44) **Note:** *Heimann clarifies that "out of it" is "doubtless miswritten for "out of the loan."")*

Cantillon should also be credited with his observation on monetary origins of inflation and income redistribution. Cantillon's observations on price differentials were revived by von Mises in in his landmark *Theory of Money and Credit* (1912) (Heimann: 43). Implications for *rates of return on the cost of living* of individuals (RRCOL) were detailed in Part II.

David Ricardo (1821) clarifies the distinction between the rate of interest and rate of profit: "The rate of interest, though ultimately and permanently governed by the rate of profit, is however subject to temporary variations from other causes." (Ricardo: 297)

Expanding upon the concept of rates of profit and interest in the context of monetary expansion Ricardo elaborates:

"(I)f by the discovery of a new mine*, by the abuses of banking, or by any other cause, the quantity of money be greatly increased, its ultimate effect is to raise the prices in proportion to the increased quantity of money; but there is probably always an interval, during which some effect is produced on the rate of interest." (298) Later Ricardo states (363) that the interest for money is "not regulated by the rate at which the Bank will lend, whether it be 5, 4 or 3 per cent., but by the rate of profits which can be made by the employment of capital, and which is totally independent of the quantity, or the value of money." (363)

*Note that at the time, precious metals as money meant that a new mine could bring additional quantities of money into the economy after the miners had covered their costs of production. The increased quantity of money would be expected to raise the prices of goods and services *relative to* the more abundant precious monetary metals.

Interest Rate Gap: Bank Lending Rates vs. Rates of Return. Ricardo makes a key observation as to the difference between what he calls the *market* rate of interest, *dependent upon the rate of profits*, and bank *business loan interest rates* for businesses as independently offered by the banking system. (Note that in this section *rates of return* and *rates of profit* are treated as essentially synonymous although further refinements could be made; also note that *lending rates* also can be referred to as *borrowing rates*).

Ricardo continues that regardless of how much banks lent, "...they would not permanently alter the market rate of interest; they would alter only the value of the money which they thus issued. ...The applications to the bank for money, then, depend on *the comparison between the rate of profits* that may be made by the employment of it, and *the rate at which they are willing to lend it*. If they charge less than the market rate of interest, there is no amount of money which they might not lend –if they charge more than that rate, no-one but spendthrifts and prodigals would be found to borrow of them." ... "The reason, then, why for the last twenty years, the Bank is aid to have given so much aid to commerce, by assisting the merchants with money, is because they have, during that whole period, lent money below the market rate of interest..." (364) (italics added)

Knut Wicksell (1898), in a view attributed to the marginalist approach to value and distribution, viewed the *natural interest rate* and the *rate of profit* as *equal*: The "...average or natural interest rate is equal to the real rate of return on capital, i.e. the general rate of profits...." (Panico: 195, and 45 citing Wicksell, English translation 1965, pp132-134)

Wilhelm Ropke (1936) in reference to Wicksell speaks of the equilibrium rate (of interest), or the "real rate of interest" in Wicksell's sense, as the "...equilibrium rate in the economic system which is only a fictitious figure reflecting roughly the average rate of profits anticipated from capital investment...." The term "average profit expectations," "profit expectations" and "profits on capital" are mentioned in the context of booms and credit inflations, caused by a widening of the *gap* between the rate of interest and profits on capital. (1936: 114-115)

Later in the 20th century, James Grant (1996) describes a similar gap: "When the yield curve is positively sloped, as it was in 1993, a low federal funds rate promotes bond speculation. The definition of a too-low rate ... is one set below the *expected rate of return* on capital investment. (291)

In summary, based on the classical specification of a general relationship between the market/natural interest rate and the rate of profit/return highlights a critical "interest rate gap" emerges: When banking institutions lend at rates that are "too low" -- meaning below the general rate of profits/natural rate of interest, then excessive borrowing/lending may result, with later disruptions in markets due to overproduction and oversupply (gluts), malinvestment and the like.

The analytical framework of the interest rate gap likely remains relevant into the 21st century, although at some point in the early 20th century the concept of an "interest rate gap" nearly vanishes in mainstream discourse.

Additional Commentary: Wicksell may not have used the term "market" interest rates. In the 20th century, due to monetary interventions, interest rates can no longer be considered as based on rates of return in the classical sense. Modern interest rates therefore termed "policy interest rates" in this book and in Kennedy (2015). Ricardo's term "market" interest rates could possibly be renamed to free market interest rates--based on rates of return, not policy.

Perhaps the term "natural" interest rate is designed to highlight the concept of interest rates based solely on rates of profit and excluding rates influenced by monetary policy or bank lending rates.

The statement that the rate of profit and natural interest rate are *equal* may be intended to describe an equilibrium state. However, in practice it may be more precise to suggest that free market rates of interest move roughly in tandem with rates of profit (i.e. the movements may mirror one another, but the rates themselves are not equal).

The Interest Rate Gap: 20th Century Disappearing Act?

Overview. As of the early 20th century, there were two distinct forms of interest: Market/natural rates of interest deriving largely from rates of profit (rates of return) and "loan rates" (rates of interest charged by banks/the banking system). In the classical view a "gap" between the two rates can lead to lending excesses if loan rates are below natural/market interest rates.

*Ricardo used the term "market", Wicksell and others following him referred to *natural, equilibrium* or *real* interest rates, as noted above (Wicksell 1898, Ropke 1936).

Discounted Cash Flow (DCF) Analysis and the Discount Rate. As discounted cash flow (DCF) analysis and bond pricing were integrated into economics in the early 20th century, a departure from the classical view may have arisen. Fetter may have conformed to the classical view in his discussion of discounting: Recall from Part I that Fetter (1914) stated that the discount rate was determined through an estimation process by enterprisers (entrepreneurs) as to the affordability of interest, but not necessarily as the interest rate itself.

From some point forward the internal rate of return (IRR) appears to have been called the *interest rate* (re: Fisher's *rate of return over cost* and Hotelling's research on exhaustible resources); this was covered briefly in Part I under the topic of the *internal rate of return* (IRR). A notable example of the interest rate usage was in the context of bonds, as detailed in the following section.

Interest Rates and Bond Financing.

The use of the term "interest rate" in the context of bonds and bond financing (i.e. *yield to maturity* or *internal rate of return*) also may have caused some confusion regarding any previously posited relationship between interest rates and rates of profit.

Bond pricing was discussed in Part I in the topic of applications of the internal rate of return (IRR). Recapping here: "If (the) bond is traded, and a market price is therefore available for it, *the internal rate of return* can be computed for the bond—that is the discount rate at which the present value of the coupons and the face value is equal to the market price. This internal rate of return is called the *yield to maturity* of the bond." (Damodaran: 398)

Expanding upon the work of Bohm-Bawerk (1901) and the theory of time preference, Irving Fisher (1906, 1907, 1930) refers to the subject of discounted present value in *The Nature of Capital and Income* (1906). Capital value was defined there "...as the discounted present value of a future income stream..." and *"(T)he rate of interest* was the price linking the flow of income with the stock of capital value." (Backhouse: 155). (Italics added)

Fisher's monumental research may have resulted in highly significant departures from any classical approach to interest deriving from profit and the concept of the "interest rate gap."

First, the "interest rate" becomes linked to bond financing in the sense of *yield to maturity/discount rate* in bond valuation.

Second, *profit* is moved into the category of *risk* rather than as an element of the interest rate. The topic of "risk and uncertainty" is detailed in Part I [re: Frank Knight (1921)].

The end result appears to be that interest is no longer viewed as a derivative of profits in the classical sense and any gap between market/natural interest rates and loan interest rates of the banking system ceases to exist.

On the first point, Fisher (1930) what is also called the *internal rate of return* (as in *yield to maturity* of a bond, abbreviated as YTM) appears to have been referred to as the "interest rate." For instance, after noting the principle that market prices represent discounted benefits Fisher clarifies the determinants of bond pricing as: "...*the rate of interest* to be realized and the series of sums or other benefits which the bond is going to return to the investor. Aside from risk, there can never be any other factors in the calculation except these two." (Fisher 1930:17) (Italics added)

The term "interest" is applied widely as a determinant of market* value: "...all property and wealth---stocks, land (which has a discounted capital value...), buildings, machinery, or anything whatsoever. Risk aside, each has a market value dependent solely on the same two factors, the benefits, or returns, expected by the investor and *the market* rate of interest* by which those benefits are discounted." (1930: 18) (Italics and asterisk added)

In sum, "... it may be well here to point out that interest is not, as traditional doctrine would have it, a separate branch of income in addition to rent, wages and profits." Fisher also provides a footnote that includes a reference to Fetter (1914) on interest theory (Fisher: 32-33).

*Note: An asterisk is added to the term "market" above to highlight a possible definitional difference: A problem with referring to "market" (as in "market value" or "market rate of interest") is that the "market" rate of interest used in discounting to present value may be considerably influenced by *non-market factors* originating in monetary policy; see the discussion elsewhere on *policy interest rates* and the *riskfree* rate; also Kennedy (2015). Therefore, a key distinction should be made between this usage of the term "market" and the classical sense (re: Ricardo, Wicksell).

Profit

Fisher (1930) deals with profit in two ways. First he tends to reject the idea of relating profits to the term "interest": "...Much less would it be worthwhile to call enterpriser's profits interest. No one ever attempted to capitalize them. But in meticulous theory, all may be capitalized and so become interest." (34)

Second, he associates profits with *risk*: "As to profits, I believe that the most fruitful concept is also that of the man in the street. When risk attaches to any one of the aforementioned forms of capital -- human beings, land, houses, pianos, typewriters and so forth--the man in the street calls the net income profits."(33)

Historical Significance

Whether as the result of the loose use of language, or by intent, this transformation away from the classical "interest rate gap" may have cleared the way for a stronger debt-orientation of the economy, in which centrally controlled interest rates by the monetary authorities through *policy interest rates* could influence borrowing rates and bond values; the greater the perceived value of bonds the more financing through debt for organizations (including firms and governments alike) in pursuit of economic stimulus and desired growth objectives.

APPENDIX 4

Returns and Interest Rates in Growth Theory

Special mention is made of the general equilibrium model of John von Neumann because of the inclusion of a form of profitability (and unprofitability) into the model (von Neumann 1945). Moreover, general equilibrium models remain in use for economic analysis at the policy level, such as *computable general equilibrium models* (CGEs) and *dynamic stochastic general equilibrium models* (DSGEs); (Dixon and Jorgenson, 2013, Romer 2012, Solow, 2010, Wickens, 2011).

Von Neumann's celebrated contribution to growth theory, *A Model of General Economic Equilibrium* (1945), attempts to merge the interest rate and economic growth: The *interest factor* β is equated with the *coefficient of expansion* α. The tentative conclusion that the "real growth rate of a dynamic economy should equal the real interest rate in long-run equilibrium." (Klein 1983: 125)

A notable feature of Neumann's model with regards to the subject of *rates of return* are the *technical variables*—variables for *intensities of production, x_i* and a common factor α, the *coefficient of expansion** of the whole economy. The technically *most* *efficient* intensities of production are assumed to be brought about by the normal price mechanism. If there is a loss, i.e. P_i is *unprofitable,* the intensity $x_i=0$, and that particular productive process P_i is not used. "The problem is to establish which processes will be used and which not (being "unprofitable"). (1) When equilibrium is reached, profit is no longer made on any process P_i, otherwise prices or the rate of interest would rise. (Von Neumann 2-3)

Commentary

A few points of interest concerning model assumptions are noted here.

Profit. Although the model assumes zero profit in equilibrium, a question arises whether in an equilibrium state there are any possible scenarios in which positive rates of profit could exist that would not cause prices or the rate of interest to rise.

Regarding subsequent research and modifications to von Neumann's general equilibrium model that relaxed the assumption that all profits are saved, Backhouse (1987) states "...it followed that the rate of growth was equal to the rate of interest multiplied by the fraction of profits saved." (322)

Say's Law. The model's structure suggests that "(I)t is impossible to consume more of a good G_j in the total process than is produced." (Von Neumann: 3)

Interestingly, this bears some similarity to Say's Law: "One can only buy with what one has produced," and "the one product constitutes the means of purchasing another" [Say (1803) as cited by Hutt (1974: 25)]. Hutt also provides statements from James Mill (1808) that not only clarifies the meaning, but also suggests that the principle is the source of national wealth through *production and productive activity*: "The collective means of payment of the whole nation...consist in its annual produce" and "(A) nation's power of purchasing is exactly measured by its annual produce." [Mill (1808) as cited by Hutt (1974)]. For additional references on Say's Law, see Sowell (1973).

Inequalities and Solvability. Von Neumann was careful to point out the model's shortcomings. The model is comprised not of equations, but of "rather complicated" *inequalities* "... the fact that the number of conditions is equal to the number of unknowns

does not constitute a guarantee that the system can be solved."
(Von Neumann: 3) In his notes to the text, von Neumann states:
"It is, incidentally, remarkable that (*) does not lead—as usual—
to a simple maximum or minimum problem, the possibility of a
solution of which would be evident, but to a problem of the saddle
point or minimum-maximum type, where the question of a
possible solution is far more profound." (Von Neumann: 5).

APPENDIX 5

Models, Probability Theory and Normality

In statistical analysis and in econometric modeling, estimates for
the arithmetic mean of various financial measures are generally
assumed to follow an approximately normal distribution. The
central limit theorem provides a basis for the normality
assumption, and roughly stated, relies upon the outcomes being
generated additively and by numerous small independent
processes.

It is worth considering whether rates of return (and other financial
measures) may at times be influenced by a dominant external
force relative to other impacts, and whether some processes may
not be entirely independent. Economic theory briefly referenced
in the main text may help provide some clues; a particular area of
interest is whether underlying monetary and financial system
dynamics may exert an "abnormally" significant impact on
economic activity.

Therefore, some form of normality testing could be a useful
supplementary tool of analysis. A better understanding of
probability distributions and economic dynamics may be in order.
Accordingly, attempting forecasting and constructing forecasting
models without consideration of the normality assumption could
produce questionable results.

APPENDIX 6

Cash Flow Effects of Asset Purchases with Debt and Equity

Capital expenditures are a component of cost in the derivation of
net cash flow (NCF), net net cash flow (NNCF) and rates of return
on cost (RRC) as detailed in Part II. Since these costs are cash

outflows, it is helpful to clarify the cash flow effects of purchases of fixed assets (such as machinery). Of particular interest is the case where equipment is financed with debt or equity; it might be argued that there is no *cash outflow* involved. The following example illustrates what happens from a generalized accounting standpoint.

Cash Purchase. Suppose that in fiscal Year 2016 a company decides to purchase a new 3-D printer to replace a broken one, and has sufficient cash resources to pay cash for the purchase. This new 3-D printer will be added to PP&E, net, by the acquisition cost (purchase price) of the printer. This change is also reported within *capital expenditures* on the company's *cash flow statement*. These capital expenditures (also sometimes abbreviated as *Capex*) are part of the *Investing* section of the cash flow statement, and are record as an *outflow* of cash. Note that while the P,P&E account increases, the cash account is expected to *decrease* by the same amount, and since both are assets, then there is *no net increase* in total assets on the balance sheet.

Financing with Debt or Equity. If the equipment is financed with debt or equity, it might be argued that there is no *cash outflow* involved in the purchase. The journal entries below should clarify that a cash outflow still occurs in order to purchase the equipment

Suppose that a firm seeks financing to purchase a new 3-D printer in a given fiscal year. The cash can be obtained by either borrowing (increasing debt capital), or by increasing equity capital by contributions from investors or the owner(s). In both cases, *cash inflows* occur in connection with the financing; recall that these inflows are not revenues of the firm, they are *financing* inflows.

Increase in Debt Capital. For an equipment loan (financing through an increase in debt capital):

    P, P&E x
                    Cash......................x
    Cash.................x
                    Equipment Loan.........x

Cash is received in the form of a loan (an increase in debt or liability), and then the cash is used to pay for the equipment. The assets increase by the amount of the cash paid, and the *debt capital* increases by the amount of the loan.

Increase in Equity Capital. With financing through an increase in equity capital the generalized entries could be:

$$P, P\&E \ldots\ldots\ldots x$$
$$Cash\ldots\ldots\ldots x$$
$$Cash\ldots\ldots\ldots x$$
$$Capital \ldots\ldots\ldots x$$

Note. For a first-time equity capital "raise" the equity could be in the form of an *initial capital contribution*, *private placement* or an *initial public offering* (IPO). Equity can be raised for various types of entities, such as start-up businesses or other entrepreneurial business ventures. An interesting historical example for a new venture in agribusiness is provided by David Ricardo (1821) who on the subject of reduced rates of profit states "...and on those terms only could a new farmer with 6000 *l*. money in his pocket enter into the farming business." (Ricardo: 122)

Subsequent additions to equity capital can also be in the form of *capital contributions*, *private placements* or other types of *equity issuance*. On the balance sheet of the enterprise an *addition* to equity capital would appear as an increase to the Equity account; the cash flow statement will show the amount contributed as a cash *inflow* to the business; again recall that this is *financing activity* not the result of sales.

APPENDIX 7.

Future Directions for Economic Management

This appendix summarizes some analytical tools that could serve as a resource for investors, businesses and policymakers alike. It is assumed that these tools could be applied without the need for changes in the current institutional framework.

Investors and businesses may be able to benefit from a better understanding of the possible mispricing of assets and investments. Policymakers in the pursuit of "growth" however defined, may also hope to avoid disruptive financial and economic crises through more effective tools of economic management.

Interest Rate Determination: The *interest rate gap* of the classical view may be difficult to measure in practice, but *credit-based interest rates* as proposed in Kennedy (2015) may offer a relatively simple approach for lending institutions to compute interest rates but firm-by-firm and on a *firm-specific* basis that could help reduce the likelihood of over-indebtedness/overlending leading to subsequent financial and banking crises and economic disruptions.* Firm-specific interest rate data could potentially be aggregated to provide an indicator of industry-wide and economy-wide trends and central tendencies, although credit-based interest rates should be viewed as originating with the credit analysis and creditworthiness of individual firms. *Note: Although not covered in Kennedy (2015) credit-based interest rates could be further improved upon by taking into account *uncertainty* of net cash flows; also see the commentary in the Appendix regarding normality and probability theory.

Monitoring of Asset Valuations. When purchasers of assets, whether homeowners purchasing a residence or savers investing for retirement suffer losses and/or negative equity in their homes, the consequences can be devastating. Rates of return, specifically the rate of return on cost (RRC), could be an alternative measure towards better monitoring of asset valuations. Analysis of returns-to-asset valuations (abbreviated as a "returns-to-valuation analysis") can be applied to identify possible "gaps" in various asset markets and asset mispricing in real estate, securities markets (equities and debt securities) and elsewhere. Recall the analyses of income real estate and equities in Parts I and II. An additional point concerns *wealth inequality*, which may persist when the price growth of assets systematically exceeds the growth in rates of return of financial entities.

Monitoring of Price Inflation. When annual consumer price growth outpaces annual growth in the rate of return on the cost of living (RRCOL) greater financial hardship for consumers may occur due to loss of purchasing power. Additional study of a rate of return on the cost of living (RRCOL, i.e. the "return"), and a "returns-to-consumer price gap" could therefore be helpful in monitoring price growth.

For individuals, knowledge of the RRCOL may be useful in understanding the importance of comparing higher incomes to the potentially *higher* cost of living—and therefore a possible reduction in living standards.

Low Returns and Poverty: Countermeasures
Sources of poverty through declining purchasing power are noted above. In addition, the current low rate-of-returns environment also may limit the income-generating potential of individuals. While it may be agreed that savers should be rewarded with current income for saving, higher returns often depend on capital appreciation or higher-risk investments such as *junk bonds*; but after adjusting for risk of loss—i.e. *risk-adjusted returns*--the returns may in fact be *lower*.

Proposals to offset lower incomes due to low returns may come with serious drawbacks, such as "reflating" the economy through more debt-based growth; concomitant rises in nominal policy interest rates may in *real terms* not be sufficient to offset inflationary impacts, while continuing to cause hardship for those on fixed incomes. Another challenge of raising policy interest rates in the absence of a guide as to where interest rates should be, is the possibility of an *excessive* rate increase that could be unnecessarily damaging to the economy. As just noted above, the topic of credit-based interest rates (Kennedy 2015) is an attempt to provide a framework; the computation of interest rates would be on a firm-specific basis (but aggregation of firm interest rate data could serve as a guide for policymakers). While certain financial entities (firms) are incapable of servicing their debts at higher interest rates and may require *restructuring*, others may actually be quite capable (See Kennedy 2015). If the credit markets ever began to reflect scarcity of capital, some firms are likely to have sufficient debt service capacity from net cash flow to pay *higher* interest rates when bidding for loan capital. In turn, these higher rates would provide higher rates of return for financial institutions, savers and investors. The process would have to be managed very carefully, however, because in the current paradigm many firms have become debt-dependent.

Cost-saving Technologies and Real Incomes. Technological advances in various fields and in particular *energy* hold a

133

potentially game-changing key to reducing costs for financial entities (whether organizations/businesses or individuals). Therefore, as detailed in Part I of the book, despite a *nominally* low-returns environment, if costs overall are *declining* at 2% per year, *real* incomes are in theory rising. A rise in real incomes potentially unlocks savings that did not exist before and is a form of "return" in terms of greater purchasing power. While many technologies already exist, they may not yet be cost-effective enough for widespread commercial use. Therefore, commercialization of cost-saving technologies is also part of the process of poverty reduction.

Entrepreneurship. A possible solution that may require some rethinking of certain policy interventions in markets is *entrepreneurship*. The formation of new businesses provides individuals not only with a set of valuable skills and a chance to become financially self-sufficient, but can provide income-- not only to the entrepreneurs but also for those they may employ as well as investors (including the entrepreneurs themselves). Since the risks of failure of start-ups are very high, gaining experience and guidance from a variety of sources including retired professionals, online and other educational programs that provide specialized training and/or hands-on experience to develop entrepreneurial and management skills are key. Part of gaining experience early is freeing up time to take on entrepreneurial projects; online education may be particularly helpful in this regard. A new business concept may not necessarily require starting from scratch: The purchase of *existing* businesses and properties (e.g. income real estate) are options as well, but also require serious study and preparation.

An objection might be that added competition from new businesses could hurt existing businesses. This is possible, although new business niches can be developed while transacting with *existing* businesses to create and add value. The concern of excessive competition is acknowledged but an important cause-- excessive *financing*—is often overlooked. Lax lending practices/overlending can result in a debt-based oversupply of highly similar types of enterprises that after a period of fierce competition can fail in clusters (re: malinvestment).

Alternative Valuation Approach?

Rates of return on cost may also provide a measure that can be used as an alternative discount rate in valuations in addition to standard measures that involve *estimation* of the discount rate discussed in Part I of this book. The appropriate rate of return measure should be firm-specific and relate to the valuation of the particular firm or possibly the same industry. Moreover, the rate of return measure would ideally be adjusted for uncertainty of cash flows, so that an *expected rate of return on cost* or E (RRC) measure could be developed; long-term historical data would also be preferable. The degree of uncertainty involved should also take into account non-normality and economic factors that could cause sudden shifts in cash flows. See Appendix 4 regarding probability theory.

Re-evaluation of Economic Growth Measures. Economic growth is typically defined as GDP growth in the national income accounting framework. It could be generally agreed upon that national income accounting has its foundation in producer microeconomics (e.g. business activity). As stated by the OECD (2014):

"Because the corporate sector, particularly non-financial corporations, is the largest contributor to value added, corporations are viewed as the backbone of economic growth in most developed countries." (OECD 2014: 114)

What, specifically forms the backbone? It could reasonably be argued that without some level of positive rates of return, firms will be in a weaker position to provide additional employment opportunities, or increase purchases of goods and services, capital equipment, real estate and other assets.

It is considered here that rates of return on cost both for organizations/firms and individuals/households could be considered as an alternative measure of economic performance, although not necessarily entirely satisfactory from a proactive, results-oriented policy standpoint due to natural unpredictability and the possibility of volatility and inconsistency from year to year.

135

Some fundamental problems with GDP as a measure of economic performance ("growth") are considered here. First, *value added* when considered alone neglects the fundamental concept of the *costs incurred* to generate the value added. If value added is rising, but associated costs are rising faster, the economy may be described as "growing" nominally, but the rate of returns relationship suggests a worsening. Second, when GDP "grows" annually, the growth that is measured is relative to the value added of the previous year --but the value added is analogous to a *gross* measure of profit rather than a *net benefit* (aka *return*) measure. Third, GDP accounting tends to be circular, as in a circular flow of income; it would seem reasonable that an accounting system should in some way reflect drivers of economic behavior. Profit-loss accounting can be a starting point, and a rates of returns framework may further refine such an accounting approach. If it can be assumed that a key driver of behavior of many firms as well as individuals is to increase their *net benefit* relative to the *costs incurred* to generate the net benefit-- i.e. a continued drive towards reducing costs-- then rates of return on cost may be capable of capturing this dynamic. Recall the law of accelerating returns (Kurzweil 2001) from Part I.

Conversion Exercise. It may be possible to reconfigure the relevant data so as to convert national income accounts into a measure of RRC for a hypothetical "national" financial entity (firm). An initial and rudimentary attempt is made in the following example.

The table below shows a hypothetical national income accounting from the expenditure approach and the income approach perspectives. Note that the value added from each approach, 20, should equal one another. Capital consumption allowance is also referred to as "depreciation" and could be a proxy measure for capital expenditures of firms.

Expenditure Approach	
Value of Output	100
Less: Interfirm Purchases	80
=Value Added	20

Income Approach	
Wages	8
Interest	1
Rents	1
Business Taxes (indirect)	2
Capital consumption allowance	3
Taxes on Business Profits	2
Dividends	1
Undistributed Profits	2
Valued Added	20

Costs. From a business standpoint, we now identify each cost category before interest and profits: Interfirm purchases (from the Expenditure Approach), then Wages, Rents, Business Taxes (indirect), Capital consumption allowance, and Taxes on business profits.

Net Benefit (Return). The items that constitute the firm's net benefit/surplus is dividends, interest* and undistributed profits. *Note that interest is to be deducted later as part of the financing costs of the business.*

The result, revisiting the Net Benefit Accounting Framework from Part II, is shown here:

NET BENEFIT ACCOUNTING FRAMEWORK

Revenues (Value of Output)	100
LESS: Cost of Production (Cash Outflow):	
Cost of Goods Sold (COGS)	80
Selling, General & Administrative (S,G&A)	9
Capital Expenditures (Capex)	3
Acquisitions,other	4
Subtotal-Cost of Production	96
=Net Net Cash Flow (NNCF) *	4
Less: Dividends/Distributions	1
NNCF -D (Source of Repayment for Debt Se	3
Less: Principal Repayment (P)	
Less: Interest Payment (i)	1
NNCF after Debt Service	2

*Note: NNCF is the *net benefit*, *return* and can also be referred to as *equity income* (Kennedy 2014). The term "value of output" is added alongside *Revenues* to indicate the GDP framework from which the data originated.

Rearranging the GDP data, we now have revenues of 100, cost of 96 and a *net benefit* or *return* of 4 (=100-96). The *rate of return on cost* (RRC) for that fiscal (or calendar) year is therefore about 4.2% (=4/96). This figure could be reviewed annually as a rough measure of economic performance. Should the evidence be supportive, rates of return dynamics could also be given consideration for integration into economic models given recent criticism of their applicability to real-world phenomena (Solow 2010).

However, it should be noted that rates of return for individual firms are potentially quite volatile, and cannot be expected to increase constantly year after year, which may be disappointing from a growth-oriented policymaking standpoint. This does not imply that rates of return should artificially be manipulated upwards in order to "stimulate" the economy, because such manipulations may simply involve the removal of resources from elsewhere/others in various ways including through inflationary means.

Nevertheless, the year-to-year *change* in the rate of return can be computed and compared to asset valuations as in the *returns-to-valuation* analysis detailed in this book. Fundamentally, "economic growth" may be an overly misleading term to describe economic activity. Rates of return on cost may be a useful alternative measure of economic "performance" if only to reflect the drive to economize on resources so as to generate a *net benefit*, (whether in the form of positive net cash flow (NNCF) for businesses or in savings by individuals). Despite probable future attempts to inflate currencies in hopes of rekindling "growth" through additions of debt ("debt-based growth"), we also are likely to experience continuous technology-driven "shrinkage" in terms of savings through cost reductions—in short, economization.

ADDENDUM

Conventions attempted in the book are mentioned here, although it is recognized that these conventions may not always be consistently applied. **Parentheses.** When a term appears in parentheses after another term [such as *creditors (lenders)*], the meaning of the two terms is taken to be very similar but possibly used in different contexts. The use of "i.e." within parentheses is designed to emphasize the term. "E.g." within parentheses is an abbreviation for "example" as in "for example." Also, "aka" is an abbreviation for "also known as"). Occasionally parentheses will be used in front of or behind another to mean that the word is optional but can help clarify the meaning. **Slashes.** A slash (for example, debt/borrowings) means that both terms are considered to be nearly identical in meaning and therefore "joined" together by a slash. **Italics** are added because of its deemed importance and often to indicate a common term in the field that could be researched elsewhere for background information. **Boldface** is intended usually to indicate a subtopic. **Currency Units** are at times stated (such as dollars) when necessary, but when a neutral example is provided that involves currency, the term "currency units" may also at times be used. **Quotation marks** are used either for emphatic effect, for a popularized term, informal jargon or common expression used in a particular field, industry or context. **References.** It can be difficult to cover economic topics without referring to research that might have fallen out of the mainstream, or that is unpopular with certain groups. It was decided that the popularity of a particular view should not necessarily be a basis for inclusion or exclusion of a particular body of thought. **Citations.** If the same work is cited in succession, the same work may be indicated only by enclosing the page number in parentheses; it is assumed that the same work is being cited. A number of citations are sourced from another researcher. It is recognized that a particular citation may not be representative of, or fully convey, the entirety of a body of research and therefore can be misleading if not qualified. Moreover, it is not unusual for some historical writings be confusing or inconsistent. It is understood that some educated guesswork may be necessary at times to ascertain what an author most likely intended to say, as even scholars in the field may be unable to fully agree on the meaning of certain passages.

REFERENCES

Abramoviz, M., "Resource and Output Trends in the United States since 1870," *American Economic Review*, Papers and Proceedings, May 1956.

Alesina, Alberto and Giavazzi, Francesco (Eds.), *Fiscal policy after the Financial Crisis*, National Bureau of Economic Research (NBER), University of Chicago Press, 2013.

Backhouse, Roger., *A History of Modern Economic Analysis*, Basil Blackwell, Inc., 1987.

Badger, Ralph E., *Valuation of Industrial Securities*, Prentice-Hall, 1925.

Barro, Robert J., "Are Government Bonds Net Wealth?", *Journal of Political Economy* (Vol. 82, no.6), University of Chicago, Nov/Dec 1974

Bauer, P.T., *Equality, the Third World and Economic Delusion*, Harvard University Press, Cambridge, Massachussetts, 1981.

Becker, Gary., *The Economic Approach to Human Behavior*, Chicago: Chicago University Press, 1976.

Borio, Claudio., Erdem, Magdalena., Filardo, Andrew., Hofmann Boris., "The Cost of Deflations: A Historical Perspective," *BIS Quarterly Review*, March, 2015.

Bohm-Bawerk, E. von., "The Function of Saving" *Annals of the American Academy of Political and Social Science* (May, 1901).

Brealey, Richard A., and Stewart Myers., *Principles of Corporate Finance*, The McGraw-Hill Companies, Inc., 1996.

Cairncross, A.K., *Factors in Economic Development*, London, Allen and Unwin, 1962.

Cantillon, Richard., *Essai sur la Nature du Commerce en Général (traduit de l'anglais)*, 1755.

Christ, Carl., "A Simple Macroeconomic Model with a Government Budget Restraint," *Journal of Political Economy* 76 (1) (Jan/Feb 1968), 53-67.

Christ, Carl., "On Fiscal and Monetary Policies and the Government Budget Restraint," *The American Economic Review* 69(3-5) (1979), 526-538.

Cobb, C. W.; Douglas, P. H. (1928). "A Theory of Production". *American Economic Review* 18 (Supplement): 139–165.

Cohen, Jerome B. and Zinbarg, Edward D.., *Investment Analysis and Porfolio Management*, Richard D. Irwin, Inc., Homewood, Illinois 1967.

Coltman, Michael M., *Buying & Selling a Small Business*, International Self Counsel Press, Ltd., 3rd Ed., 1991.

Damodaran, Aswath., *Investment Valuation.*, John Wiley & Sons, Inc., 1996, (3rd Ed.) 2012.

De La Calle, L.S., (1544) *Instruccion de Mercaderes* ... (part trans. in Grice-Hutchinson 1952)

Denison, E.F., *Accounting for US Economic Growth 1929-69*, Washington, Brookings Institution, 1974.

Devajaran, Shantayanan, and Anthony C. Fisher., "Hotelling's Economics of Exhaustible Resources: Fifty Years Later," *Journal of Economic Literature* Vol. XIX (March, 1981), 65-73.

Dewing, Arthur Stone., *The Financial Policy of Corporations*, 5th Ed., The Ronald Press, 1953.

Dixon, Peter B. and Jorgenson, Dale., *Handbook of Computable General Equilibrium Modeling*, Volume 1A, Elsevier North Holland, 2013.

Dorsey, Pat., *The Five Rules for Successful Stock Investing: Morningstar's Guide to Building Wealth and Winning in the Market*, Morningstar, Inc., 1994.

Fetter, Frank A., "Interest Theories, Old and New," *The American Economic Review*, Volume IV, No. 1 (March 1914), 68-92.

Fisher, Irving., *The Rate of Interest* (New York: Macmillan, 1907).

Fisher, I., *The Theory of Interest (as Determined by Impatience to Spend Income and Opportunity to Invest It)*, New York: The Macmillan Company, 1930.

Friedman, Milton., *Price Theory*, Walter de Gruyter: Aldine Publishing Company, 1986.

Gordon, M., *The Investment, Financing and Valuation of the Corporation*, Richard D. Irwin, Inc., Homewood, Illinois, 1962. (Gordon Growth Model)

Grant, James., *The Trouble with Prosperity*, Times Books/Random House, 1996.

Grice-Hutchinson, M., *The School of Salamanca: Readings in Spanish Monetary Theory, 1544-1605, 1952.*

Harcourt, G.C and Laing, N.F., (eds) *Capital and Growth*, Harmondsworth: Penguin, 1971.

Heimann, Eduard., *History of Economic Doctrines*, Oxford University Press, 1964.

Hicks, J.R., *Value and Capital,* 2nd Ed., Clarendon Press, Oxford, 1946.

Hitchner, James R., *Financial Valuation: Applications and Models*, 3rd Ed., John Wiley & Sons, 2011.

Hollingsworth, Barbara. "Economist Tells Congress: U.S. May Be in 'Worse Fiscal Shape' Than Greece," *CNS News*, March 9, 2015.

Hotelling, Harold., "The Economics of Exhaustible Resources," *The Journal of Political Economy* 39 (2) (April, 1931), 137-175.

Huerta de Soto, Jesus., *Money, Bank Credit and Economic Cycles*, Ludwig von Mises Institute, 2012.

Hutchison, Terence., *Before Adam Smith: The Emergence of Political Economy* , 1662-1776, Basil Blackwell, Ltd., 1988.

Hutt, William., *A Rehabilitation of Say's Law*, Ohio University Press: Athens, 1974.

International Monetary Fund, "United States: Selected Issues Paper," *IMF Country Report* No. 10/248, July 2010.

International Monetary Fund, "*IMF World Economic Outlook (WEO)*, April, 2015.

Keynes, John Maynard., *The General Theory of Employment, Interest, and Money* (1936).

Kennedy, Raoul., *Equity Income Analytics*, Amazon Publishing, LLC, 2014.

Kennedy, Raoul., *Interest Rate Analytics*, Amazon Publishing, LLC, 2015.

Klein, Lawrence R., *The Economics of Supply and Demand*, Basil Blackwell Publisher Limited, 1983.

Knight, Frank., (1921) *Risk, Uncertainty and Profit*, LSE reprints of scarce tracts, London, LSE [as cited in Backhouse (1987) and Friedman (1986)].

Kurzweil, Ray., "The Law of Accelerating Returns," (kurzweilai.net/the-law-of-accelerating-returns), March 7, 2001.

Kuznets, Simon., *Modern Economic Growth: Rate Structure and Spread*, New Haven, Yale University Press, 1966.

Lucas, Robert (1976). "Econometric Policy Evaluation: A Critique". In Brunner, K.; Meltzer, A. *The Phillips Curve and*

Labor Markets. Carnegie-Rochester Conference Series on Public Policy 1. New York: American Elsevier. pp. 19–46.

Malthus, Thomas. (1815), *An Inquiry into the Nature and Progress of Rent*, as cited in Winch (1987) Oxford University Press.

Manhattan Institute for Policy Research, "Hutt: An Economist for This Century", *Manhattan Report on Economic Policy*, Vol III No. 5., 1983.

Markowitz, H.M.,"Portfolio Selection," *The Journal of Finance* 7 (1): 77–91, March, 1952.

McCormick, Liz., "Global Bond Rally Near 'Panic' Level with Japan Yield below Zero," *Bloomberg Business*, Feb 9 2016.

McKinsey Global Institute, "Debt and (Not Much) Deleveraging," *MGI Report*, McKinsey & Company, February 2015.

Mill, John Stuart (1848)., *Principles of Political Economy*, Books IV and V, Penguin Group, 1988. (Original 1848)

Miller, Merton H., and Charles W. Upton., "A Test of the Hotelling Valuation Principle, " *Journal of Political Economy* 93 (1), 1985.

Mises, Ludwig von., Economic *Calculation in the Socialist Commonwealth* (original: "Die Wirtschaftrechnung im sozialistischen Gemeinwesen", Archiv fur Sozialwissenschaften 47 (1920)), Ludwig von Mises Institute, 2012.

Mises, Ludwig von., *The Theory of Money and Credit* (translated from the German,1912), 1934.

Moody's Investors Service Global Credit Research, "Putting EBITDA in Perspective," *Special Comment*, June 2000.

Neumann, J.V., "A Model of General Economic Equilibrium," *The Review of Economic Studies*, Vol. 13 No.1 (1945-46), pp 1-9.

OECD, *National Income Accounts at a Glance*, Organisation for Economic Cooperation and Development, 2014.

Panico, Carlo., *Interest and Profit in the Theories of Value and Distribution*, The Macmillan Press, Ltd., 1988.

Peters, Josh., *The Ultimate Dividend Playbook*, John Wiley & Sons, Inc., 2008.

Piketty, Thomas., *Capitalism in the Twenty-First Century*, Harvard University Press, Cambridge, Mass., 2014.

Pratt, Shannon P., *Valuing a Business*, 2nd Ed., Business One Irwin, 1989.

Ricardo, David (1826)., (P. Sraffa, Ed. with M. Dobb)., *The Works and Correspondence of David Ricardo, Volume I: On the Principles of Political Economy and Taxation*, Cambridge: Cambridge University Press, 1951-1983.

Romer, David., "Dynamic Stochastic General Equilibrium Models of Fluctuations". *Advanced Macroeconomics* (Fourth ed.). New York: McGraw-Hill Irwin, pp. 312–364, 2012.

Ropke, Wilhelm., *Crises and Cycles* (adapted and revised by Vera C. Smith), William Hodge and Co. Ltd., 1936.

Rosenbaum, Joshua, and Joshua Pearl., *Investment Banking: Valuation*, Leveraged Buyouts and Mergers & Acquisitions, (2nd Ed.), 2013.

Ross, Stephen., "The Arbitrage Theory of Capital Asset Pricing". *Journal of Economic Theory* 13 (3):341–360, 1976.

Schilt, James H., "A Rational Approach to Capitalization Rates for Discounting the Future Income Stream of Closely Held Companies, " *The Financial Planner*, Jan., 1982.

Sigurjónsson, Frosti., *Monetary Reform: A Better Monetary System for Iceland,* Reykjavik, Iceland, March 2015. (Report commissioned by the Prime Minister of Iceland, Edition 1.0, 2015)

Say, J.B., *Traité d'Economie Politique*, 1803.

Scott, Maurice FitzGerald., *A New View of Economic Growth*, Oxford University Press, 1989.

Serra, Antonio (1613)., *A Brief Treatise on the Causes which can make Gold and Silver Plentiful in Kingdoms where there are No Mines*, cited in Hutchison (1988) from Monroe A.E. (1924) *Early Economic Thought*.

Shultz, Theodore W., *Distortions of Agricultural Incentives*, Bloomington, Indiana University Press, 1978.

Schumpeter, J.A., *History of Economic Analysis*, 1954.

Shim, Jae K., Siegel, Joel G., and Simon, Abraham J., et al., *The Vest-Pocket MBA*, Prentice-Hall, Inc., 1986.

Solow, Robert., "Capital Theory and the Rate of Return," in Harcourt, G.C and Laing, N.F., (eds) *Capital and Growth*. Harmondsworth: Penguin, 1971.

Solow, Robert M., "Technical Change and the Aggregate Production Function," *Review of Economics and Statistics*, August 1957.

Solow, Robert., Prepared Statement of Robert Solow, Professor Emeritus, MIT, to the House Committee on Science and Technology, Subcommittee on Investigations and Oversight: "Building a Science of Economics for the Real World," July 20, 2010.

Sowell, Thomas., *Say's Law*, Oxford University Press, 1973.

Smith, Adam (1776), *An Inquiry into the Nature and Causes of the Wealth of Nations*, David Campbell Publishers Ltd., 1991

Stigler, George J., *The Theory of Price*, 4th Ed., Macmillan Publishing Co., 1987.

Stockman, David., *The Great Deformation: The Corruption of Capitalism in America*, PublicAffairs™, 2013.

Stockman, David., "Soon Comes the Deluge," *Contra Corner,* January 19, 2016.

Tuller, Lawrence W., *The Small Business Valuation Book*, Adams Media, 1994.

Walker, Francis A., *Political Economy*, Henry Holt and Company, New York, 1888.

Wicksell, Knut., *Geldzins und Guterpreise, (Interest and Prices)* Jena, 1898 (English-language translations 1936, 1965: Interest and Prices, New York, Kelley 1965).

Wickens, Michael., *Macroeconomic Theory: A Dynamic General Equilibrium Approach*, Second Edition, Princeton University Press, 2011.

Winch, Donald., *Malthus*, Oxford University Press, 1987.

OTHER RESOURCES

Annual financial statements of the firms in the study were sourced from the filings with the U.S. Securities and Exchange Commission (SEC) or from company annual reports containing financial statements. The NASDAQ, Wikipedia, Wikinvest, Econ Library (econlib.org) and Yahoo Finance websites were consulted for financial and other information.

www.ingramcontent.com/pod-product-compliance
Lightning Source LLC
Chambersburg PA
CBHW070245190526
45169CB00001B/312